Whistleblower

Abuse of power in the church – a New Zealand story

TANDEM PRESS

For all the women who have suffered
and who have gone unheard.

But let justice roll down like waters
and righteousness like an ever-flowing stream.

Amos 5.24

First published in New Zealand in 2001 by
Tandem Press
2A Rugby Road
Birkenhead, Auckland
New Zealand
www.tandempress.co.nz

ISBN 1 877178 78 0

Cover design and illustration by Magma Design
Text design by Verso Visual Communication
Production by *Book*NZ
Printed in New Zealand by Astra Print Ltd

Contents

Acknowledgements

I want to take this opportunity to acknowledge with gratitude all of those people who have been involved in this continuing saga over nearly twenty years. To those who continued to support and listen in the spirit of friendship, providing emotional and spiritual counsel, thank you, for without it this story could never have been told.

To those who have not been able to last the distance but were there in the beginning, many thanks for carrying me when I could not walk.

To those who have supplied legal counsel, I cannot thank you enough for your clarity of judgement in a situation where there was none, for your ability to guide us with a steady hand into a position of dignity and control.

To the Board of Governors of the college, thank you for being prepared to review the situation ten years later. Thank you for removing the portrait from the wall and standing firmly in support of the women against the male clergy who complained about its removal. Thank you for organising the meeting with the Primate and the Bishop and for sitting alongside in supportive and protective silence while we put our case forward. You offered us redemption at the same time that you redeemed yourselves and for this we thank you.

Thank you to Bob Ross and all those at the Tandem Press – I appreciate the stand that you have taken. Thank you too to Jeanette Cook who kept asking the tricky questions and to Jane Hingston who, with her mind for detail and her ability to present the very best, has carefully put it all together. I hope that your faith has been justified!

Foreword

This is a courageous book and one that needed to be written. It is an exposure—a personal exposure of great daring on the part of the author, Louise Deans, of the sexual abuse to which she was subjected when she began her ordination training for priesthood in the Anglican Diocese of Christchurch. To her great horror, she eventually discovered that many of her female colleagues had been similarly abused.

It is also an exposure of another kind: the blatant unwillingness, hostility and resistance of the church's hierarchy and its reluctance to want to know about it, believe it and confront it.

It is not surprising that it has taken so long for *Whistleblower* to be written. It is nearly twenty years since the initial events occurred, but the nature of those events were so traumatising, required such painstaking soul-searching and intensive healing, that until that took place writing could not commence. Even then I believe it would have been an agonising and scary book to write.

As I read it I found it difficult to comprehend and believe that what was being revealed—sexually abusive acts and attitudes of the most degraded and degrading kind—took place within what is supposed to be the safety of the Christian community. What is especially remarkable about the book is Louise Deans' ability, in the face of all she endured, to have distanced herself from those acts and attitudes sufficiently to reflect upon them both psychologically and theologically and to produce a document that stems from her disciplined and intelligent mind.

Hopefully, the most important thing about *Whistleblower* will be the change it will bring about within the life of the church. I refer here to all branches of the church. Perchance that process has already begun. As I reflected on my reading of it, I was strangely reminded of C.S. Lewis describing himself, on the occasion of his conversion in Trinity Term of 1929 at Oxford, as the most 'reluctant convert in all England...kicking, struggling, resentful, and darting his eyes in every direction for a chance of escape'. Now that Louise Deans' book has brought light to this dark and sinister corner of the inner life of the church there will be no 'chance of escape' for the church. It must ensure that no such behaviour occurs again, or should it occur again, that it will deal with it very differently.

C. Arthur Mitchell
BA (NZ), MA (Cant), DipTheol (Knox Dunedin), MNZPsS
Minister Emeritus, Presbyterian Church of Aotearoa New Zealand
Registered Psychologist
Psychotherapist

Preface

The main events of this extraordinary story took place between 1981 and 1993. The incidents related here might not appear extraordinary to the women who have experienced sexual abuse in secular male-dominated professions. What was unusual here was that the events that took place happened in the church. However, in light of the recent media coverage of sexual abuse within the church to women and children, this is evidently not unusual. I was one of the women involved in these revelations and I believe it is important to record these events, which led to significant changes to the constitution of the church. The events related in this book illustrate the kind of power that male priests can have over women in the church. The power which was exercised in this instance became sexual abuse.

The primary aim of the women who reported these incidents of sexual abuse, by submitting complaints as required under the canons and statutes of church law, was to protect other women who might find themselves in similar situations while they trained for the priesthood, as well as the women students who were about to enter a university college that until 1989 had been for men students only. The second aim of the women was to ask the church to take appropriate steps to ensure that all women were guaranteed protection from sexually predatory male priests. The third aim was that justice should be seen to be done, and the fourth aim was to ensure that all women in the church were educated to understand and be able to deal with the pervasive and insidious syndrome of sexual abuse disguised by power.

I have decided, in this book, not to name the perpetrator or many of those involved, even though they have been named in the daily and weekly newspapers. The women who put forward their complaints about sexual harassment have always desired anonymity. The reason for this is that the church remains a patriarchal institution where the women can still be blamed and punished for revealing the inappropriate sexual behaviour of predatory male priests and it is important that they continue to be protected.

Introduction

This book has been very painful to write. Yet it must be written because so many people were traumatised over and over again by the process. It is now more than a decade since the stories of sexual abuse in the Anglican Diocese of Christchurch were revealed. Over these last ten years there has been time to reflect deeply on the stories the women told about how they had been subjected to acts of sexual abuse and about the way the church handled the complaints they subsequently laid against the perpetrator of this abuse. The male priest in question at that time held many senior positions within the church and was the principal of a university college.

I thought that all of this had been laid to rest, that the events had been left behind us and we could get on with the rest of our lives. But matters that have not been properly handled have a habit of rising up again and again until they have been understood for what they are, confronted, proper procedures followed, and a final and appropriate vindication made. It was made very evident to me that this matter had not been settled for good and for all when recently I dined at the aforesaid university hall and saw, to my consternation, that the portrait of the principal who had sexually abused and harassed me and other women had been hung on the wall of the dining room of the college in a black and white chronology of principals who had served their time there. To have this man gazing down at me while I was eating caused a choking sensation in my gut. It was, to say the least, a most disconcerting and uncomfortable experience. I felt very strongly that his portrait did not sit well on the wall among the other principals—upright and astute men of faith who had served well their church and their God. I thought that the other principals depicted alongside him were tainted by his perversity and perversion. I dared myself to look up at the picture of this man who had been my tormentor for so long. His face and bearing looked as enigmatic as his personality and his life had been when I had trained for ordination under his direct supervision. I wondered why the board of governors had hung his portrait there, considering all the events that had taken place ten years before.

At the dinner, I talked about my feelings of abhorrence to two of the current board members who were present and I also approached the present principal of the college. One of the board members was as concerned about it as I was; the other requested that I talk to the vice-chancellor of the university, who was also present, which I did. The present principal told me that the issue about whether or not to hang the portrait had been debated at a board meeting and the board had decided to hang the portrait. He added that the portrait of President Nixon hung alongside the other portraits of the presidents of the United States. I was rather puzzled by the implication that if it was all right to hang the portrait of President Nixon then it was equally all right to hang the portrait of the Reverend Canon R alongside the portraits of the other principals. I expressed some bewilderment at his argument, but I was led to believe that the bad must always sit alongside the good. It is both a philosophical and a theological debate; for the church does recognise this dualism of good and evil. However, when the church itself harbours the perpetrators of evil and protects them at the expense of the people whom they are called to serve, then we have a possible anomaly in the argument. This dualism between good and bad also raises issues for other institutions, all those that have the ability to turn a blind eye to bad behaviour within their ranks and to protect those who are employed to serve the institution but who are in reality using the institution for their own ends.

This is a difficult and complex story about a difficult and complex man who worked within the ranks of the church and who was protected by the church in spite of many complaints laid against him by women who had suffered sexual abuse and harassment at his hands. The question that needs to be asked is why the church ignored the women's complaints and protected the very man who was using the church for his own nefarious activities. Or, in more general terms, to ask why the church harbours individuals who seek to have power over others and who use this power to fulfil their own perverted needs by preying on the vulnerabilities of others. The power that is conferred upon its workers is a spiritual power, one that is contained within the church structures and is meant for good. However, this power can turn on itself and become a tool used to fulfil an urge for self-gratification. This is when it becomes a perverted and negative power that seeks to destroy.

When the hero speaks, he utters in the full light of day what he has learned in the dark; he reveals what has been covered beneath the public rhetoric of praise and promise, makes known what has been hidden beneath the mystifications of the élites, proclaims clearly what has only been whispered among the élites and their retainers. He describes the master for what he is, and acknowledges the fear of his power. The whistleblower is no fool. He realises that he will pay a price, but he has decided to accept the cost rather than continue to pursue his exploitive path.

The servant faces a problem. He has blown the cover story and disclosed the real story, but he has acted alone. He has no support for his action. Having broken his solidarity with the other retainers, he has nowhere to go. Consequently, when he denies the self he was becoming, he is cut off from the land of the living. Because he has been an oppressor, he will receive little sympathy or support from peasants and other rural poor. He acts alone, and he is vulnerable to aristocratic wrath. As long as whistleblowers act alone, they can be handled. When one acts alone, one dies alone.

William R. Herzog II, The Vulnerability of the Whistle-Blower: The parable of the talents. Matt. 25:14–30; Luke 19:11–27, *Parables as Subversive Speech*, ch. 9, pp. 166–7. Westminster/John Knox Press, 1994.

ONE

The road to ordination

Before I start, I want to tell you a little bit about myself and my life experiences before I applied to be a candidate for ordination training. The reason for this is to offer some background about who I am in the context of my family, what I have done with my life and where I have been. I want to tell you some of the critical points of my life that have shaped me and guided me towards the church as my destination. Perhaps a less obvious reason for this self-revelation is an inner anxiety that I may be perceived as not being 'street-wise', as being naïve. Maybe I am, but I think that many of us are naïve when we are confronted by crises that are outside our experience. In my own defence, therefore, I want to say yes, I can be naïve, and yes, I am vulnerable; but at the same time I am also a 'woman of the world' and I have not been totally protected from its dangers and desires. If I have to accept the criticism of privilege, then I would accept that only if privilege means a secure and loving childhood, a good education and the opportunity to live out of New Zealand for nearly six years.

I was brought up in the small provincial city of Timaru in Canterbury, in the South Island of New Zealand. I was born the third daughter in a family of four girls and one boy, the ham in the middle of the sandwich. My father was a doctor, well-loved by all his patients, and my mother was a glamorous, beautiful woman, dominating and lively, who gave us a strong sense of family, community, a sense of fun and the desire for adventure.

We were the baby boomers, the post-war babies who proliferated and swarmed into the world, swamping the kindergartens and the primary and secondary schools by our sheer weight of numbers. We arrived in great droves of young hopefuls, the offspring of husbands and wives who had been forced apart by the Second World War and who wanted to make the most of their time together after having lived for so long in the face of death and despair. We were the outward and visible signs of their inner hope that we would have a better life than theirs, but we did not understand that then.

But now we do. Now we understand why we were to be kept as white and as pure as the driven snow. For we were the ones who were singled out to be the creators of a society that would be free from war and poverty, where everyone would live side by side in peace and plenty. To this end, hundreds of us were sent off to Sunday school, to church and to Bible class. Later, we sang lustily like angels in the church choir and taught Sunday school ourselves. We hungered and thirsted for righteousness, whatever that was. We longed for salvation, but did not bother much to think what we were to be saved from exactly. We were kept on a tight rein as far as boys went, and any adolescent friendship with a boy was frowned upon as though boys belonged to another race, one that we should not mix with. So boys were imbued with an enticingly mysterious quality.

After a tumultuous and crowded primary school where we were crammed fifty to a classroom and where I learnt more about life than I ever let on to my parents, I was sent to a small private secondary school where professional careers were not encouraged. The ethos of the school seemed to be more oriented to marriage and motherhood than careers. I remember one Sunday when I was sixteen years old, after I had taught the children at Sunday school and sung in the church choir, I engaged in a conversation with the curate, who questioned my interest in the church. He saw church as a crutch for the elderly—especially those who had lost their spouses—not for the young. It seemed to me that I was being told to go and live a little before I needed to be a regular church attendee and maybe I even needed to sin a little in order that I might be forgiven. I mounted my bicycle and never returned.

I struggled against the odds to go to university. As the third daughter I was expected to trail along the deep rut ploughed for me by my two older sisters. My eldest sister had gone to university without success although she is an accomplished musician. The second eldest undertook nursing training. When I stepped forward and announced that I wished to go to university, however, I was tarred with the brush of my eldest sister's failure. In order to subvert me away from such a dangerous and profligate desire, my parents offered me some alternative suggestions for a career. One of these was that I attend a home science school, where I could learn the delicate art of household management, how to make beds and how to cook. This was not what I had in mind at all. I wanted to read English and languages, Latin, Greek and French. I was not destined for domesticity. I insisted that I be allowed to attend university. It was the first time in my life that I had ever insisted on anything, and it precipitated a crisis. My parents finally relented and I was duly escorted to Christchurch to enrol at the University of Canterbury.

In order that I might be safe, I was placed in an Anglican hall of residence for young women. Chapel in the garage was compulsory every Sunday. I stayed there for two years before I was allowed to go flatting with friends. It was at the beginning of my second year that I met Jim, and we did everything together for three years before we were married at the age of twenty-one, after we had both graduated.

Within a short time we had jobs and money that we could call our own. We used this to do what most other people did at our age, which was to fly away from New Zealand for our big overseas experience. Jim took up a position as assistant solicitor in a law firm in Lincoln's Inn Fields in London and I was accepted into London University to do a post-graduate diploma in library and information studies at University College. I gained employment in the Kensington Public Library on the condition that I would stay in their employ for a minimum of two years and not get pregnant during that time.

These conditions proved to be untenable. Jim was asked by his law firm if he would like to take up the position as legal advisor to the finance minister of the government of Bahrain, a small kingdom in the Arabian Gulf. We were in the 'why-not' phase of our lives and it seemed like an exciting adventure to set off for an unknown and mysterious destination.

We were well briefed for our expedition. It was an exhausting and dangerous place to live where the heat soared some days to 128 degrees Fahrenheit in the summer, and the Arabs would always have a gripe about something and would let off some bombs from time to time. It was considered to be a hardship posting for many of the Europeans on the island. We were told that we would either love it or hate it. The story was related to us about the man who arrived at the airport and hated it so much that he returned to London on the next plane back. I was to fall into the category of people who loved it with a passion that can only be had for the desert.

✣

When we arrived in Bahrain I was eight months pregnant, having breached my contract at the library. My father, doctor that he was, had said that giving birth to a baby was a natural function that could be done anywhere; even, he said, under a palm tree. He added the story about the woman on horseback who dismounted to give birth to her baby and then rode on and caught the others up. I did not think I was quite as hardy as that; but on his advice, I decided not to stay in London or travel out to New Zealand for the birth, but to go to Bahrain with Jim and have my baby under the proverbial palm tree.

The conditions in the maternity hospital were primitive.

There was no air-conditioning, only a languid punkah that revolved slowly and merely stirred up the hot air. In the delivery room there were three plastic curtains separating the beds. My legs were tied firmly into 'stirrups' and, while I was giving birth to my daughter, I learnt about the status of women in Middle Eastern culture. I was not permitted to know the sex of my baby until I had passed the placenta. The reason for this is because daughters are called 'mistakes' and if the woman giving birth knew that she had given birth to a daughter she might retain the placenta, preferring to die rather than face the wrath of a husband who only wanted sons. The ruler of Bahrain, Sheikh Isa, told us that he had seven sons and five mistakes, meaning daughters. This attitude towards women permeates the whole culture and is endorsed by Allah in the Holy Koran.

The fundamentalism of Islam was evident all around me. I did not have to read a book to discover how women are treated by the men in the Middle East. What I thought at first were black plastic rubbish bags on the streets were in fact women squatting on the footpath dressed in their black nylon, heat-absorbing abbas. Their faces were hidden from view by a black facemask made from goatskin or plastic, which had two slits for their eyes to see out. The more wealthy women wore gold coins around their facemasks, and these tinkled when they moved like a bell around the neck of a cow. The girls were married off at puberty—about twelve or fourteen—often to men who abused them, and they would be pregnant before they had finished their childhood. One woman aged twenty-eight had fourteen children. This was an eye-opener for me.

The Muslim religion influences and dominates the daily lives of all its citizens, including telling them when to get up in the morning and when to go to sleep at night. Islam shapes and controls the Arab culture to a degree that would violate human rights in a Western civilisation. And yet it is quite fascinating to be part of a culture that is suffused and permeated with religion.

My first contact with Islam occurred when we had just arrived in Bahrain and I was lying on my bed exhausted by the heat and puffed up with oedema. I was very frightened to see an Arab man dressed in scruffy work clothes with a dirty white cloth wrapped around his head bobbing up and down outside my bedroom window. Time after time he would appear, stand for a moment with his head down and then he would disappear again. He kept going up and down, up and down, and I had no idea what he was doing. When I realised that I was not the object of his scrutiny, and that he was deeply engaged in something other than being a peeping tom, I rose from my bed intrigued, tip-toed over to the window and peered out to see what on earth he was doing. There he was lying barefoot and prostrate on his prayer rug on the veranda, out of the sun, praying to Allah. His shoes were lying beside the rug. I understood his preoccupation and was not afraid any more.

I became used to the daily call of the mullahs from their towers; they would compete with each other to announce the start of a new day at the exact moment the sun rose, when the sun was at its zenith, or when the sun had set, and in between, at morning and afternoon tea time. I enjoyed the cackling, cacophonous loudspeakers, which pitched the moaning prayer over the people in the barastis made out of date palm fronds. Synchronicity and harmony were elements they did not aspire to, and I used to laugh out loud at the coughs and splutters of the mullahs in the midst of their prayers. The daily calls of the mullahs are the one thing that I miss the most. No-one could ever feel isolated in an Arab community with the mullahs spreading the word about the glories of creation and the greatness of God five times a day whether you wanted to hear it or not. And each time, the Arab men would stop whatever they were doing, take off their shoes, roll out their prayer rug and prostrate themselves in prayer to Allah.

The religious festivals or eids were intensively lived out by the people in the community according to whether they were happy or sad eids, rather like our Christmas to celebrate a birth and Easter to commemorate a death. During a happy eid there was music in the suq, the marketplace, and a feeling of such joy that I felt as though we were walking on air. It was uplifting, exciting and exuberant. The sad eids were the opposite. It was not wise to go into the suq during a sad eid, for the atmosphere was frightening and murderous. This was when the rebels would emerge, fighting would begin and bombs would explode. We were warned by radio when to stay at home and not go into the suq.

There are two especially significant religious events on the Muslim calendar. One was Ramadan when no Muslim could eat or drink during the day between the hours of sunrise and sunset. When the sun had set, they were allowed to eat and drink and make merry for the whole night. When Ramadan falls during the summer it is a hazardous time for them. First of all they are not allowed to drink anything during the day and they become crazed by the heat and dehydrated. This is exacerbated by lack of sleep. They would stagger out into the middle of the road with no regard for traffic.

The other significant religious festival was the festival of Muhurram. No other Gulf state would allow this to take place, so all the Shi'ite Muslims, who practised the observance of this festival, would surge into Bahrain to participate. This in itself gives some inkling of the nature of the festival, which was on the extreme down side of a sad eid. I had heard about it from some friends and conceived a real desire to go. The conditions under which our European and therefore alien presence was tolerated were that we must stay quiet, remain in the same place, not take any photographs and not leave until the festival had finished. We went into the suq and found ourselves a place to sit on the footpath and waited, scared out of our wits.

The build-up to the festival had taken place in the centre of the suq for the three days prior to the event. Night and day we had listened to the wailing of the Shi'ite Muslims as they prepared for the festival by neither eating nor sleeping until they had passed beyond the boundaries of normal human endurance into a maniacal fever pitch. Only with this degree of preparation were they able to withstand the blood-letting, the self-inflicted beatings with knives and chains, the slashing of their own heads with sharpened swords to let the blood flow, the dancing of the dervishes and the sombre heart-beating, all of which was to atone for the murder that Mohammed's son-in-law had committed some seven hundred years previously.

The hospital prepared for this event too, by asking everyone to donate blood and lining the streets with ambulances for emergency blood transfusions.

The festival was an unforgettable experience ranging from intense beauty to extreme masochistic self-mutilation. I disgraced myself by fainting three times. The first time was when the ghostly column of men arrived in our street after hours of marching while they chanted 'Ya, ya, Hussein' and beat themselves hard on the left side of the chest with a clenched right fist on the last syllable of Hussein. The rhythm was hollow, hard and haunting, and it filled the air with dread and foreboding. The second time was when the men who had cut themselves on the head with their swords hove into view down the street. The blood surged from the wounds in their heads and ran down their foreheads into their eyes, down their faces and dripped on to their white robes, which were stained bright red with all this gore. A man walked backwards in front of this horrible contingent, wiping the blood out of their eyes so that they could see where they were going. Many fell by the wayside and were rushed to the waiting ambulances. I think the third time I fainted it was a way of achieving some respite from this atrocious festival of blood-letting. As I was stretched out on the footpath from the trauma of it all a kind Arab woman covered me with her abba to protect me, an alien European, from the curious eyes of onlookers.

At one level, I really envied the Muslims. They appeared to have a living faith that was acted out in daily life and in which they participated with an intensity I had never experienced before. My experience of organised religion seemed by contrast to be a wishy-washy, pallid and diluted faith, which did not have much relevance to daily life. Worship was assigned to a particular place at a particular time on a particular day. It was not lived out in the hurly-burly of daily life, nor in the intricate threads of existence, but appeared only to re-enact a piece of rather unfortunate history that had happened far too long ago in another culture to have any relevance to the twentieth century Western world. Religion seems to be more of an anachronism in the Western world, but in the Muslim religion I saw an intensity of involvement that was not just confined to Sundays. I saw a physical re-enactment of the faith story that was not just performed in ritual but lived out in a brutal reality of pain, blood and death. This was more real than anything I had ever experienced before.

After the birth of my second daughter I began to go to the Anglican church on Sundays. Going to church was my one hour off during the week when Jim stayed at home to look after the children while I had time out. During the time I attended regular Sunday Christian worship in the middle of a Muslim culture, Christianity actually began to make some sense. It was no feeble, wishy-washy religion at all. It was as intense as Islam in its intention and when it was lived out below the same Middle Eastern skies that Jesus had lived and taught under, it became as intensely real as Islam. I thought that perhaps Christianity had ultimately failed in the Western world simply because the West had a totally different climate from the East, away from the intensity of this lived spirituality in the midst of the heat, the perpetually blue skies from which no rain fell, the wadis, the date palms, the melody of the suq, the chatter and the clatter, men holding hands with other men without shame, the clarity of the atmosphere. I loved it. I was enchanted by it. And I felt sorrow for my Western world, which could reach this world neither through their culture nor through their faith.

I was welcomed into the Anglican church in Manama, the capital of Bahrain. It was a desert church, a church of the oasis, a Western Christian oasis in the midst of Islam. It was for me a place of intense learning about the religious symbols that depict existence. One day the minister asked me to take up the collection. I looked around anxiously to see if there were any men there, for in my experience only the men took up the collection in church. There were no men there, so I gathered that someone had to do it and that someone on that day was to be me. I felt greatly humbled by the honour. Another time he asked if I would blow out the candles on the altar. I hesitated and must have looked bewildered, because again that wonderful old Irish priest, who had cancer of the throat, gently insisted that I could. To go beyond the altar rails was to step into the sanctuary, the holy place that only the priest himself was allowed to occupy. It was so hard to step into that holy place that I felt as though I was pushing through a physical barrier. I did not consider that the barrier might be psychological. As I stepped through the barrier I had a strong feeling that I was dirty and unworthy to be there and I associated that feeling with the blood of my menstruation. Now I wonder at my reaction, knowing as I do that at the heart of religion is the notion of the creative blood of life and the humility to accept the life that we are given in all its mystery and unknownness.

It seems strange looking back on it now and re-living those first moments when I began to enter a spiritual self-consciousness and self-awareness, especially with regard to my sex and what women did and did not do. This was the years 1973 to 1976, and the women's movement was a burgeoning industry in the United States of America. I thought I was 'liberated', and I am sure that if anyone had ever asked me if I was a feminist I would have said

'Of course I am. Who isn't?' But there was a quantum leap between the theory and the praxis of feminism in the early 1970s compared with the 1990s; and the Middle East was not the best place in the world at that time to practise my feminist beliefs.

As well as becoming aware of blood as a religious symbolism of life and atonement for life, I also began to understand the importance of water as the basis of all life. Water is scarce in the desert and is also undrinkable. We bought sweet water from the sweet water truck that came by our house, and we even had to filter that. We could not drink the dirty, brown, brackish water that issued forth out of the taps. And while water is the basis of life, it can also be the cause of death; my older daughter nearly drowned when she was two years old, and I understood that life and death are separated by only a few minutes.

All the while we were surrounded by the desert, by the clear blue waters and skies of the Arabian Gulf. After three-and-a-half years in Bahrain we returned to New Zealand, moulded and fired in the crucible of a desert island.

✣

When we arrived in New Zealand in 1976 after nearly six years overseas, it was not easy to settle down in a country district on a farm. But it was easy to detect the similarities between rural New Zealand and the Middle East as far as the attitude towards women was concerned. I understand that this is a strong statement to make about any Western community, this was the 1970s still and I was looking through eyes that had become accustomed to the fundamentalism of the East. I was astonished to find in rural New Zealand, about an hour's drive from the city, a rampant cultural fundamentalism and a community that was ruled by the local Anglican vicar. What rural women were allowed to do was fiercely controlled by social pressure, and the rules were laid down as to what a woman could do and what she could not do, with the emphasis on the latter. For instance, it was not socially acceptable for a married woman to work for money, but it was expected that she work very hard in a voluntary capacity for the community, around the home and on the farm. A single girl was able to work in a paid job, but this was only to pass the time until she was married. When I first attended what I thought was our local church, because it was the closest, I was asked by the vicar what I was doing there when I belonged in the neighbouring parish. I had not realised that there were parochial boundaries and that we did not live within the boundaries of that particular parish but on the farthest reaches of the neighbouring parish. I obeyed the rules of parochial boundaries and attended the Darfield church.

My self-esteem dropped rapidly when I arrived home. I could see no future profession for myself and felt stuck in the country. I had two more children, one a son, and once again I was struck by the similarities with the male culture of the Middle East where a son is considered to be of greater importance than a daughter.

I was invited to become a lay reader and so I began to preach. Realising that my knowledge was limited, I was hesitant about the preaching process. I was also deeply aware that the connections that I had seen between Islam and Christianity, albeit at a very basic level, would be both foreign and unwelcome to a rural congregation. Also, for some reason I was afraid of committing heresy, even though I did not know what was heretical and what was not because I did not know the rules of Christianity or the boundaries of faith. Therefore, I concluded that if I was going to commit heresy it would be out of ignorance and, since ignorance was anathema, I began to study a little and then a little more until I was hooked on theology and how the meaning of life could be interpreted in a way that was relevant to life as I had experienced it in the Middle East.

It was then that I felt the strong pull towards ordination. It was not the most ideal time to contemplate such a move, since my baby was eighteen months old and still breast-feeding. I felt quite shocked by the strength of the pull, and so, of course, were my family and my friends. Jim was not pleased because life was complicated enough for him anyway without having this. He travelled into Christchurch every day to his law office, leaving early in the morning and coming home late at night to organise his 545-hectare farm. I thought that he could be more engaged with his children; also, I wanted something for myself that was mine, apart from the family. I delayed the inevitable for as long as possible, but in the end I felt compelled to act upon it and put it to the test.

While I had been contemplating my navel, the church had been contemplating its navel as well. Ministry itself was being reassessed, since congregations were falling significantly as the Western world rocketed into a new era. Particular interest was paid to the rural parishes, where one priest might be required to service five or six little churches in one parish, each with its own personality and style of worship. A new type of ministry had been developed in the United Kingdom called non-stipendiary, or unpaid, ministry; this was said to be exactly the same as the stipendiary or paid ministry, and Bishop Pyatt announced in 1981 that he thought that the non-stipendiary ministry could work in rural areas. However, the divisions between paid and unpaid clergy soon became apparent. In the minds of paid clergy, unpaid clergy were not 'real' priests. They also rather gloomily envisaged that the unpaid clergy would slip through the proverbial back door into paid ministry, thus depriving the paid clergy of jobs. It appeared that money was the control mechanism between the priest and the church, between the priest and his parish, and between the parish and the church.

I applied for this as yet untested, unpaid ministry, having fallen under the influence of the 'rural rules for rural women' that stipulated that a women may do only voluntary work. Some time later I learnt that at the time I had become a test-case for this ministry, a sort of ecclesiastical guinea pig.

✣

My application for ordination was finally put to the test. I grimly thought to myself that an interview for a paid job would be easier than the gauntlet of twelve interviews I underwent, including two with a psychiatrist.

My first interview was with the Reverend R, who was one of the bishop's examining chaplains as well as an advisory chaplain to the bishop, and was also the principal of a university college for men students. This college had formerly been a theological college for the training of candidates for ordination; but, some years before, this training had been centralised and ecumenised at St John's Theological College in Auckland. However, some remnants of theological education remained, such as courses for interested lay people and the training of young priests after they had been ordained and had taken up their first positions in the Christchurch Diocese. The college had also retained a wonderful theological library and a magnificent chapel.

R, the principal of the college, was well known as a charismatic figure in the church, admired and respected for his innovations in restoring theological education to the college for lay people. His task as examining chaplain was to interview the applicant first and make a preliminary assessment of suitability. If the applicant was considered by him to be suitable, the interview process was then thrown into gear with the other examining chaplains. R was called 'keeper of the gate' for those seeking ordination. If the applicant had his approval, then it was likely that the other chaplains would also give their approval for training to proceed.

Some time after this interview, when things had become very messy, I took the time to write down what had taken place at the interview. I wanted to understand the dynamics that were at play and what had really happened. I record these recollections here, aware that at the time I wrote them I was beginning to understand that this had been my first encounter with a man who was to wreak havoc in my life.

I was very nervous about my first interview. Months of hard thinking had led to this moment, and to say that it was a major step in my life was an understatement. I chose my dress very carefully—a blue linen skirt and a plain white blouse with no jewellery and no make-up. This seemed to be appropriate for my first interview.

I was thirty-five years old, a mother of four children and it was time for me to act. I climbed the steep stairs up to the office of the Reverend R and knocked at his door, full of trepidation. A voice on the other side of the door called out 'Come in' and I did. He was leaning back in his office chair with his feet crossed on his desk. He held a pipe clenched between his teeth, which belched great clouds of aromatic smoke into the close air of the room. He was talking on the telephone.

I felt as though I was intruding on a private conversation and felt embarrassed. I had expected formality. I had expected a man with short hair and a clerical collar sitting upright behind his desk waiting for my appointment. While I adjusted my expectations, I looked at the paintings on the walls and the library of books in the bookcases around the room. R waved his arm and gestured to me to be seated, so I found a chair and sat down. He continued his telephone conversation for what seemed like a long time, and I became increasingly agitated. He stared at me while he was talking on the phone. Suddenly I became aware that my skirt was too short and tried to pull it down. I took a deep breath, pulled myself together and tried to look relaxed and serene as though this was something that I did every day of the week.

When he had finally finished his conversation, R took his feet off the desk, stood up, walked around to where I was seated and stood over me, looking at me critically over the top of his glasses. I did not know whether to laugh or cry. I felt very disadvantaged and powerless in my low chair; I stood up, rather awkwardly to avoid bumping him, so that I could greet him.

R asked me if I would like some coffee. I declined. He whirled rapidly out of the room announcing that he was going to have one anyway. I had a moment of breathing space until he poked his head around the door and asked me with an engaging smile whether I was sure that I did not want to join him in a cup of coffee. I was unable to resist this second invitation and changed my mind. He called out from the little kitchen to ask if I took milk or sugar, and I answered, 'Just milk'. This proved to be a problem. He said 'Damn', stormed back into his office, picked up the telephone and told his secretary to bring up some milk. Then he rushed back out the door to make the coffee. Soon he came back into the room and paced around restlessly as though I was not there.

I heard footsteps running up the stairs, and his secretary entered without knocking and handed him the milk. He introduced me to her, and she looked me up and down coolly, said hello and disappeared down the stairs again. R disappeared with the milk and was absent for some time. When the door opened again, he was concentrating hard on the difficult operation of holding the door open with his shoulder while he manoeuvred his body plus two full cups of coffee (one with milk) into the room without the door springing back on his hands. He was only successful to a small degree, since the coffee from both cups spilt on the carpet. He swore again, shook the spilt coffee off his hands and handed me my cup of coffee, with milk. I wished that I had not recanted on my first decision. When I received the cup from him, I discovered that my hands were trembling so much that the coffee in my cup spilled into the saucer and splashed onto my white shirt. Now I felt shame as well as embarrassment. I wondered how difficult ordination would be if it took this much effort to get a cup of coffee with milk.

> R sat down behind his desk and scrutinised me with large, piercing, blue eyes. He asked me why I had come. He already knew that, so I wondered why he wanted me to tell him. I told him that I wanted to be ordained. At this, he arose from his chair again and whirled around his desk to the other side of the room. I was forced to twist my body around to see him. 'Why has it taken you so long to come?' he asked me intently. I was taken aback by this second question, which I had not anticipated. He was not to know that I had struggled with the question of ordination for a long time, that it had been hard to come out of my faith closet and expose my inner self. It was as though he was talking to my very soul as no-one had before.
>
> Neither was it easy to answer his next question. 'What is your sex life like?' he asked. Altogether, I was to have twelve interviews with the bishop's examining chaplains and a psychiatrist, and not one of them would ask me about my sex life. When I was later interviewed by the psychiatrist I was tempted to ask if questions about my sex life were normal and if so why. But I didn't. I simply could not get the words out.

I am glad that I had written this piece when I did. I had no idea where it was going, but looking at it now, and in the light of Peter Rutter's analysis in *Sex and the Forbidden Zone*, (Unwin Paperbacks, 1990) which I read much later, I can see quite clearly what the signs were.

First of all, I am not a shaker. For me to shake so violently throughout an interview that my cup spills is a strong pointer that something was happening to me. Also, I can quite happily spill coffee in my saucer or on myself at any time without feeling enormous rushes of shame and embarrassment as if my life hung upon it. As well as this there was my indecisiveness over whether I should actually have a cup of coffee or not. I regretted changing my mind when I witnessed the chaos that it caused and the inconvenience both for him and for his secretary, who had to bring the milk upstairs.

There was a lot of movement on R's part; he was pacing back and forth and rushing in and out of doors for no real reason. I think I became mesmerised by all this movement and felt as though I was being tied up, round and round my chair so that I could not move. Next was the stopping and staring as though he could see inside me. Of course he could not see inside me. How ridiculous to think that someone could do that without being given permission. And he stopped so close to my body that I was unable to move normally without bumping into him; I had to twist my body uncomfortably away from the close contact he was creating. He was violating my boundaries, badly. He thrust his body so close to mine and peered at me so intently that I was not even able to breathe.

And last of all the questions. Anyone with any sensitivity would understand that this first interview was important and that the applicant would be nervous. The interviewer need not have asked the sort of questions that he did. I mean, how does one answer questions like that? They are not questions that can be answered in a minute anyway, and certainly not until a considerable amount of trust has been built up over a period of time between the one who has the power to ask and the one who must respond to this powerful person who cradles your hopes in his hands. Hindsight is all very well, but it does not take away the fact that that first experience made me feel like I was bait for a predator.

✣

I heard on the grapevine that my application to train for ordination had been successful. A friend rang to congratulate me, but I at that stage knew nothing. I had to ring R to find out that the examining chaplains had voted unanimously for my selection. R attributed my selection entirely to his own recommendation to the selection committee. It was one more reason to be grateful and feel obligated to him. The noose was beginning to tighten.

There was one strange question that he asked me at that time. He said that he was unable to understand why the women examining chaplains had been so supportive of my application. He seemed unable to understand that sometimes women do support other women, and he asked me if I was a lesbian. I looked at him in consternation, for I thought that my four children would be indication enough of my heterosexual bias.

I was not happy about his constant references to my sexuality for several reasons. In my conservative middle-class family, sex was a taboo subject; boys were discussed at length, but not sex. That was left to basic instinct. If sex was not a topic for discussion, then homosexuality certainly was not—my family would today be considered to have been homophobic. Also, I was given the impression that R knew more about me than I knew about myself; so his asking about my sexual orientation gave him a power over me that was quite unacceptable. But I did not think that then; I was thrown into confusion and distress about my own identity. Never before had my sexuality been called into question and been the subject of such scrutiny. I could not see what it had to do with my application.

R was appointed by the bishop as my mentor and spiritual advisor. The title given to confer his status in this role was 'Uncle'—a close family member, but not as close as a father. With both a biological father and God the Father, there was too much competition for that title. An 'uncle' was close but not too close. It was his duty to guide me as a candidate in training for ordination to the priesthood, with his wisdom, knowledge, experience and maturity. To be truthful, I was delighted with his appointment as my mentor. Apart from the initial embarrassment at the first interview, which I had rationalised to be my problem, I saw him as the ideal mentor for me. He was funny, charming, conceited, egotistical and challenging. He knew theology, he knew the bishop, he knew the archbishop. He was a superb preacher and liturgist, he was the chairman of the New Zealand

Prayer Book Commission and a member of a national theological education committee for training clergy and lay people. To me it seemed that he was at the coalface of the church, he was the charismatic visionary.

He appeared to be universally admired. The wife of a vicar even told me that she thought he was 'dishy'. I ought to have been suspicious of this enthusiastic endorsement of him, but instead I felt pleased and proud that I was the subject of her envy. Another vicar's wife eagerly asked me if he had hugged me when I had been accepted for training. In fact he had not hugged me at that point, but at a later time I was to experience one of his famous hugs. I was taller than he was, and when he embraced me I patted him on the back as I would one of the children. He jerked back angrily and said, 'Don't do that.' 'Do what?' I asked innocently. He said, 'Don't pat me on the back like that.' I did not dare after this ticking off! I became the recipient of his famous hugs whenever I went into his office, behind the door, against his academic robe he would embrace me with great passion!

And me? I was eager, ambitious, curious, hungry for God and hungry for theology. I felt that I was an empty bucket that just needed to be filled up to be ready to go. But whenever I asked him for information, he would not deliver. I wanted to know who else was training for the non-stipendiary priesthood so that I could have a peer to accompany me through the training process. Nothing was forthcoming. I knew that there must be others in training, for when he handed me a book in which to record my spiritual journal he said that he had chosen the best one for me from a pile, which confirmed my suspicions that others were also given books from this pile. I asked him about my personal training programme so that I could organise my time. I was told nothing except that there were options in the pipeline, hoops for me to jump through, although he would not be specific about what these were. I asked him how often we were to meet. Again no answer was given, except to say that this would develop over time. It was a lot of rubbish really. He was not organised, there were no hoops for me to jump through and no options were presented.

Finally I went out and found my own courses to do, but when I presented my options to him he would make it difficult for me to proceed with them. He was the only person I knew in the church hierarchy, and I discovered that he liked it that way. I became completely reliant on him for information, guidance, support and spiritual direction. He had absolute power over me. His approval or disapproval of me was directly related to my ordination. Suddenly I was aware that I was in a cage, locked in. I felt as though every movement I made was watched and judged by him. I experienced an acute self-awareness; it seemed that everything that I did, whether I was with him or not, was being assessed and evaluated. I felt as though I was thrown outside myself and I was the one on the outside watching what I did and how I did it. I also began to experience a vacuum around R, an empty space with no people in it and no air to breathe.

✣

About two months after my selection, R began to make sexual advances towards me. One day when we were in his office, he sat beside me on the sofa and began to stroke my face. I told him not to do that and removed his hand. He laughed, took his hand away and put it firmly on my thigh. I removed it from there also, and at the same time I asked him to stop it. I did not yell at him. I did not hit him. I merely requested that he stop what he was doing. His sexual advances were an intrusion into what I believed to be a working relationship; I became very confused, my mind went blank and I lost the thread of the conversation completely. I felt ill at ease and most uncomfortable. And yet, and this was the strange dichotomy, I liked him very much for all the reasons that I outlined earlier. But when he added the sexual component, that really confused things. Part of me was amused that he found me, a thirty-five-year-old woman with four children, sexually attractive. For heaven's sake, what woman with four children is sexually attractive, I thought. I was exhausted and stretched to my limit. Sex was the last thing on my mind.

I was pleased with myself for having dealt with the situation as I did—being firm, appealing to reason, and leaving it at that. Adult stuff—let's be clear about boundaries, I just wanted to get on with my training. I believed that I had given him an unambiguous message that I was not interested in him sexually. But as I drove home I felt nauseous, and found myself trying to figure out what had happened.

The minute I stepped through the door, the telephone rang. It was R, solicitously enquiring whether I had made the journey home all right. I told him that I had and thanked him for his concern. I did not tell him that I felt sick, confused and uneasy. I was walking right into the trap. If I told him how angry I really felt, shouted at him, or walked out on him then there would be no ordination.

After my mind had cleared, I decided to do a bit of investigation and check him out. By this time, I knew that another woman from the country had been accepted for non-stipendiary ministry but had withdrawn from training. I wanted to know whether she too had experienced sexual advances from R. Without mentioning my own situation, I asked her as tactfully as I could why she had withdrawn. She cited family reasons and I did not pursue the matter any further with her. I rang another woman whose candidacy had not yet been finalised but who seemed to be seeing him in his office regularly. She was a solo mother with three small children and she had rented a flat within walking distance of the college. She drove out to Darfield to talk with me and, without divulging any personal information, advised me to be very wary of him because he was dangerous. Later I learned that he had sexually exploited her mercilessly and was psychologically cruel to her in that he sexually used her and at the same time had deliberately denied her access to the training programme.

Now that I was aware of his propensities, albeit without any specific details, I had to make a decision. That decision was an important one to make because it involved trust. I did not make it lightly, but I was forced into making it. I was forced into a position of having to decide to trust a man who was in a position of trust in the church but was not trustworthy in terms of personal relationships. I rationalised to myself that I had been put into his care by two bishops, who must have been aware of his character.

I did try to discuss the issue of sexuality in our working relationship with him. I even went to the extent of asking to be transferred to another mentor but he refused this request on the grounds that the only other mentor available was not good enough for me and he thought that he was the only person who could train me. Another little power play, and it trapped me again. I had made a bid for freedom from him and it had failed. So I stupidly allowed the status quo to remain, and I took what I believed to be the only possible path and submitted myself to his care.

In a very subtle way, our roles began to change. Instead of him caring about my welfare, I became the carer of his. I was a dab hand at caring for others. After all, I was a mother as well as taking on roles of leadership in my rural community as the president of the local branch of Plunket and the president of the child care centre, which included a supervisory role. I was a lay reader in the church and helped many people with their personal problems. R would confide in me about the difficulties he was experiencing with his marriage. He said that his wife was having an affair, and talked about his attempts to come to terms with divorce and the significant problem of who would get the dining table. As well as this he had a lover in Adelaide; he would show me her letters covered with big lipstick kisses, and he produced a photograph of her, which he kept hidden in his file drawer. He complained that his wife would occasionally ransack his office for evidence of his infidelities. My sympathies were aroused at his dilemma and I even offered to hide his lover's letters at my place. He gratefully accepted the offer and bundled them up tightly with string and sealed them with Sellotape so that I would not be able to read them. I hid them in the attic and thought I was doing him a favour.

I rationalised this change in our roles believing that I was being tested in pastoral care and this was part of my training. He always seemed to be exhausted and complained about how much work he had to do. I had a lot of work to do too, but that was never mentioned. I felt as though I was a nuisance, but at the same time I felt concerned that I was not getting the training that I had expected. I thought that here was this man who was my mentor, highly trained and skilled in his job, and yet I could not tap into the information and direction from him that I needed.

Sometimes when I went to his office he would talk on the telephone most of the time that I was there. If I tried to leave after an hour of sitting listening to his telephone conversations, he would wave his arm at me and tell me to wait. At other times, even though he had made an appointment, he would turn up an hour late. I had a pre-school child, no baby-sitting facilities and three other children to pick up after school. I was becoming increasingly frustrated and angry.

Eventually I contacted another woman who had trained under him for non-stipendiary ministry and I talked with her about the problem. She said that she too had experienced the same compassion for him and said that she had once invited him out to her place for lunch, where he had fallen asleep. She said that she had been pleased to offer him some respite from his busy life. I thought that this was a good idea and I invited him out to my place for lunch. I believed that if he were not so tired he would be able to train me better.

After lunch, as we were walking through the house, he pushed me against the wall of a dark corridor and began to kiss me. He pulled up my shirt and bra, then he unzipped his trousers and let them and his underpants fall to the floor, leaving his genitals fully exposed. I stared in bewilderment at the strange sight of my spiritual guide standing with his pants down around his ankles. His eyes had glazed over and he was panting with his tongue out. I stood transfixed to the spot. I had no idea what to do; all my natural impulses towards self-protection had left me. I do not know what would have happened if the telephone had not rung. I leapt for the phone and answered it, pulling down my shirt. While I talked on the phone he left his pants down. This breathing space gave me time to gather my wits, and after I had finished the call I asked him to pull his pants up.

He left soon after, and only then did I have the time to reflect on what had happened. I was shocked at the incident and began to understand the implications of any involvement with him. I considered reporting him to the bishop, but I realised that I could be held responsible for the incident; since I had innocently invited him to my house for lunch, it could appear that I had 'asked' for it. I blamed myself and took responsibility for the attack.

✣

For two weeks after this I curled up in an armchair and tried to understand the issues with which I was confronted and wondered whether I should continue with training for the priesthood. I was very sure about one thing, that he was sexually perverted, that he was crazy and that—whether I liked it or not—I was implicated. I decided to tell no-one. I realised that if I reported the incident to the bishop it would be me who would be blamed, and I predicted that I would inevitably be declared unfit for training. I thought about telling Jim. But I did not have enough support from him for this venture of mine, and I knew that he, too, would attempt to subvert my training, so once again I would be left with nothing of my own. And I desperately wanted to succeed. If I told my vicar, who was a close friend of R, he would be more likely to support his friend than me. If I told my own friends, who were very proud of me, I would feel as though I had let them down. So I decided to continue as though nothing had happened.

In hindsight, I can see that this was very stupid of me. How could I have left myself open to this? Would it not have been better to have screamed at him and kicked him where it hurts most when he assaulted me? I had enough life experience to deal with him, so why couldn't I? What was stopping me? Even now it is so hard to explain. I can rationalise my behaviour and say that I was prepared to put up with anything to achieve my goal. I could even say that I liked being liked and was taken by his attention. But it was more than that. It was outside any normal experience. I felt as though I was caught in his web like a struggling fly, and he was the big black spider lying in wait. Once I was outside normality, I lost the ability to determine right and wrong. I lost my moral boundaries. I lost my way. I had no idea who I was anymore—I was topsy-turvy, confused, mesmerised and obsessed with trying to understand what was not able to be understood. I began to sleepwalk at night, obsessed with the idea that I had lost my children and had to find them again. My nightmares were terrible and I would wake up sweating with a dry mouth. But there was still more to come. The stress was beginning to tell on my body as well as my mind. I developed lumps in the sweat glands under my right arm and there was a suspicion of cancer. I was sent to see the surgeon urgently.

✣

The day of my appointment with the surgeon, R rang before I left home and said he needed to see me urgently too, so I arranged to see him on my way to the hospital. When I arrived at the college he looked tired and grey. I thought he looked worse than I was, and so sacrificial was I that I did not tell him about my own little problem. I had given up talking to him about myself anyway, because he always turned this around and made it seem to be a weakness in me. R invited me over to his house, which was adjacent to the college, saying that he had a book to give me. The floor of the sitting room was covered in application forms from the next year's students and he was also in the midst of an Australasian three-week long mid-ministry reflection course. I wondered why I had been called in to see him so urgently. We discussed the book.

Then while I was talking he stood up, came over to me, undid his trousers and pushed his penis hard into my mouth. He held my head hard against his genitals so that I could not move. I tasted the encrusted salt of old urine as I gagged and gasped for breath. He finally released me. I felt sick, degraded and humiliated beyond belief. I left straight away and went to see the surgeon. I could not have cared whether I lived or died.

I was admitted into hospital for an operation. R did not visit me in hospital.

Eighteen years later, I have just discovered from a barrister that that kind of sexual harassment is a criminal offence. The church did not think so when we women later told the bishop and the archbishop our stories about the indecent exposure, the forced fellatio and the harassment. In fact, the archbishop said of another woman who complained that she had been violated in the same way that this was not rape and that it took two to tango. But this comes later. Meanwhile I continue with my account of the events at that time.

✥

I did not die. Often I wished that I had, for I became very suicidal. I knew I was in a deep hole and that I must fight my way out of it. As I envisage it now it was as though I was floating in a black nothingness, outside the realms of my existence. I felt as though I existed as two entities; one of these was dead and the other, physical, existence had to lug this dead floating thing along with it. Walking was painful because my legs felt like sharp swords; I kept losing my balance and falling over, and my speech would sometimes be slurred. I still had to continue with my life, and with a determined effort I forced myself to carry out my daily work. I was also determined that R would not have the ultimate power of life and death over me. I had no outside support whatsoever, but I began to develop my own inner strengths and to find my integrity, that which had been lost.

Meanwhile, R continued with his exposures—in his office, in the library, in the chapel, in other public places—but I was too tired to care any more. I just got used to it and it did not seem to matter. It even seemed sort of normal, which would indicate the degree to which I had lost all moral sense of what was right and what was wrong. It just did not matter. They say that evil is like this, you just do not care; you let things happen to you that are criminal acts, but you are so used to this that you just get it over and done with and go on. Describing this feeling is the hardest thing I know—attempting to convey the humiliation, the degradation, the obsessive hatred for oneself and the man, the suicidal thoughts, the bad dreams, the desperate sleepwalking. I can assure you it is an awful place to be.

There were very few warning signs for R's attacks. One moment he would be a peaceful, funny, pipe-smoking guy and the next minute he would become a mesmerising, whirling dervish. He always took me by surprise, and I never had the ability to run away. His surprise tactics caused constant tension in me. I never knew when he was going to ring, when he would call in or when he would ask me to go and see him. Sometimes he would ring five times a day to tell me that he loved me, and then he would not ring for a month. When he rang me he would simply say hello in his rich fruity voice; but if I rang him I would have to clearly state who I was, otherwise he seemed to have no idea who he was speaking to. If he rang and I was not at home he would be very angry; but he did not tell me when he was going away. He could pay me surprise visits; but I had to make an appointment to see him. Sometimes I would muster up some strength and confront him with his irregular behaviour, his sexual attitudes towards women, but he did not seem to care. He would just puff away on his pipe and laugh at me.

Why did I persist? God only knows. But I have come across a story that seemed to make sense in these circumstances and perhaps might explain why I hung in there. The story is told of a man who is walking by the banks of a raging river. He sees a tree that has fallen into the river and at the end of the tree he sees a man in the water doing something. He calls out to the man and asks him what he is doing. The man replies that he is rescuing a scorpion to stop it falling into the river and drowning. The man standing on the bank tells him that the scorpion will sting him with his tail and he will be hurt. The man rescuing the scorpion replies that it is the nature of the scorpion to sting and it was his nature to save. Therefore it was his job to save the scorpion in spite of the continual pain that the scorpion inflicts upon him. I suppose I saw myself as that man rescuing the scorpion even though it was causing him great pain. The other text that I held on to was the gospel story of the Good Samaritan rescuing the man lying on the side of the road who had been beaten up by robbers. The similarity between these two stories is the image of rescuing, and I suppose that is what kept me in there. I had lost my sense of self—I certainly had no self-esteem—so I went for the self-sacrifice option.

✣

One day during a church service taken by the local women for international peace day, I found it hard to stay in the church.

When the vicar's wife told me that the vicar wished to see me, I bolted from the church and went to see him. Crying, I told him about my quandary, although I did not tell him about the sexual assaults. Finally I had told someone and it was a relief. Although he was friendly with R he did give me his sympathy and gave me the satisfaction of muttering 'the bastard' under his breath. When I had calmed down we discussed the option of reporting R to the bishop. However, the vicar was aware that R was doing valuable work in the diocese, and he expressed concern about R's family, in the belief that they needed to be protected. In the final analysis, he said that it was best to say nothing and leave the women to deal with it.

Nevertheless, the most important thing for me was to have told someone. It clarified things for me and I resolved to change the way I operated. I learnt that the only way I could survive was to be myself, to be honest with myself and to learn to handle the power imbalance. I became aware that I did not really know who I was because I had always tried to be the person that someone else wanted or expected me to be, and this had begun back in my early childhood. So, instead of reacting to R's moods and petty tantrums, I tried to maintain my own sense of self in spite of what he threw at me. In order to have some control in a situation where there was none, I resolved to do to him whatever he did to me. If he rang me, I rang him. If he visited me at home, I visited him at home. If he gave me a present, I gave him a present. I was determined to exercise some control by trying to create an equality, which I realise in retrospect was never possible. But at least it was a small attempt. R did not expect equal treatment, and this piling up of obligations became inconvenient for him. I hoped that by reflecting his behaviour back at him he might get the message that if my behaviour was inconvenient for him, then his was inconvenient for me. It was a dangerous game to play with a dangerous man.

As my feeling of control increased, so did my feelings of anger become clearer. No-one was going to treat me like this. Who did he think I was? I was no punching bag for his convenience. There is a saying that it takes a thief to catch a thief and if that was what it took then I was prepared to do it. I was not sure what his game was, but I had to learn it.

The results were interesting. Because I had changed and had become less eager to please, our training sessions changed. I began to plan my own training programme. The first course of training that I undertook was a clinical, pastoral education programme at a hospital for the mentally ill. R was reluctant to allow me to do this course even though he had gone over to the USA to do such a course himself. In spite of his protests, however, I applied and was accepted to do the course. It was the perfect course for me at the time—no wonder he had been reluctant for me to do it. I learned about the difference between appropriate and inappropriate behaviour, how to detect mental illness and how to really hear what is going on in a conversation. I was able to experience at first hand the manipulative behaviour of people who were mentally ill. My hunch that R's manipulative and inappropriate sexual behaviour was a mental illness was now confirmed in my mind.

I gained the confidence to confront him and to request that he be more moderate in his behaviour. This only succeeded in intensifying his demands on me. I read a book by Anne Wilson Schaef called *When Society Becomes an Addict* (Harper & Row, 1987) and I learnt about the syndrome of addiction—the secrecy of the addicted person, the denials, and the inability to take responsibility for one's actions. I now knew that the Reverend Canon R was addicted to sex just as another might be addicted to alcohol or drugs. This explained his manipulative behaviour, the vacuum of secrecy surrounding him and why so many people protected him.

The second decision I made to train myself was to study for a theological degree away from Christchurch so that I did not have to continue seeing R or be dependent on him for training. It was one way of side-stepping the increasingly bitter and confrontational relationship that had developed between us. Without his permission, I enrolled for a Bachelor of Divinity from the Presbyterian Knox College in Dunedin, which I could study from a distance. R was not encouraging of this move either, and persuaded me to test my academic ability on diploma of theology papers first, before I undertook to do a post-graduate degree. He arranged courses at the college around the papers that I was taking, to ensure my presence there. Often he would leave notes with the lecturers telling me that he wanted to see me urgently, or else he would ring and tell me to come in before the lecture, and then would prevent me from going to my lecture. I tried to study at home; but I did need help, especially with Greek. I told my Greek tutor that I was experiencing problems with the principal and that this made it too difficult for me to come to the lecture. He offered to tutor me at his flat where I could be safe. However, I could not afford to pay for my own tuition, and R refused to pay the tutor for my lessons. He told me that if I wanted to continue with Greek then I had to come to the college, and if I did not turn up at the college he would ring me to see where I was.

One day I got really angry and told him that I did not want to see him any more. He accused me of making unilateral decisions without consulting him. Every time I saw him we argued, and I could not understand why. The conversation was always manipulated by him to come around to his needs. I asked what he wanted of me and he laughed scornfully. He would not take responsibility for his own actions, nor did he seem to care about his position in the church or the college.

Eventually I told a friend about R's obsessive behaviour towards me. She told me that she had another friend, a lecturer at the university, who came to his lectures. This friend had complained to her about a sexual encounter with R when he had cornered her one night in the library after a lecture. I rang this woman and we had lunch together. She said that there was no doubt as to his intentions, and I was ready to believe her. She also said that she had given up going to his lectures in order to avoid him. She was very tactful and did not probe me for any information about my circumstances. She suggested that he be publicly confronted about his behaviour at a gathering of women.

At that time I also talked more openly with another friend who was also training for non-stipendiary ministry. She lived on the West Coast at Hokitika, and we arranged to meet half way at Arthur's Pass in the middle of the mountains. We walked through the native bush to the Bridal Veil waterfall and talked about the situation. Over lunch she asked me why I did not tell the bishop. It did seem to be the obvious thing to do, but for some reason I was hesitant about taking this course of action. This bishop did not approve of the non-stipendiary ministry, and I did not trust him to take my side against R. It was the word of an ordinand in training against one of his senior clergy. The odds were that he would push the matter under the carpet and find a way to prevent my ordination.

At this point I resolved not to take any action until after I had been ordained a priest. Even though I was finding it easier to talk about it with my friends, I was still unable to talk to anyone about the sexual assaults. I had not yet reached the stage where I could relate the sordid reality of my situation.

I even sought professional help from a member of the Anglican Care Team, who was also a priest. I told him about this tangled and confusing relationship without giving him any details of the sexual assaults. He informed me that the type of behaviour I had described to him was commonplace for men in the church and that he himself had engaged in similar relationships. He said that there was nothing wrong with it, in fact it was rather fun. This was not helpful and I became even more aware how much these men were in a position to exploit their clients to fulfil their own needs.

I even went to the psychiatrist who was on the team of examining chaplains. Once again I was unable to explain the full extent of the abuse and, even though I was very tearful, she told me that this Don Juan behaviour was a common syndrome. She assured me that there was nothing to worry about and in spite of this tangled and difficult relationship I should carry on with training. I did hope that as a member of the bishop's examining chaplains, she might report the situation and initiate some action. Later I understood that the nature of confidentiality in the counselling setting would not have allowed her to report back to the bishop.

I began to ask the other churchwomen if they had experienced sexual abuse from R. I had to choose the time and the place where I asked them very carefully since I now knew that women were reluctant to divulge information about unpleasant sexual experiences. Every woman I asked admitted that she too had experienced R's sexual advances to one degree or another. Their experiences had ranged from telephone harassment to sexual assault. As we talked over our shared experiences we began to realise that we were the tip of the iceberg. There were probably many more women all over New Zealand who had been sexually molested by him. We also understood that more women would suffer his addictive and predatory behaviour if he were allowed to continue any longer. The most serious problem, we felt, was the fact that young women students were about to be admitted into the college. Some of the women I was talking to revealed that they had been sexually assaulted by R when they were young students at Auckland University, where he had been the Maclaurin chaplain. If he was a predator then, how serious would his offending be now with the female students.

I also tried to tell Jim what I had been experiencing. Again I could not tell him the total story and so his reaction, which was to shrug his shoulders and turn away, was quite understandable. He said that I just had to learn to deal with it. I remonstrated with him and told him that it was beyond my control and that I did not know how to deal with it. He still showed no comprehension, so I gave him a practical demonstration—I lunged at him the way R lunged at me. Jim winced and bent over to protect himself, and backed away from me with a look of fierce indignation. I said to him that that was what I was experiencing and that I did not appreciate the attacks either. I informed him that there was a group of us who wished to report the matter. With that he turned to me and said that if I did I would be sued for libel. At this point I decided to say no more about the matter so that I would at least have home as an oasis where I was free of the problem.

✣

Once I had made contact with other women who had suffered in a similar way, the big picture began to come clear. I had suspected that I was only a small part of a much larger problem, and this suspicion proved to be true. I was not surprised. I only felt relief that I was not on my own any more. There was no doubt that R was a sex addict and that no woman was safe under his care, or even in his presence. Several of us set up a warning system whereby others who were coming into the college could be alerted that there could be a potential problem with R's sexual advances. We decided among ourselves who we would warn and set about doing so. We wrote to other women who were engaged in professional working relationships with R. We put the word into the network of churchwomen throughout New Zealand. Many more shocking and tragic stories emerged.

In the meantime, in 1990 the board of governors of the college had decided to admit women students. We realised that there could be great danger for them and for the reputation of the college if R were to remain as principal. It had been revealed to us by several victims of his rapacious sexual appetite, that, as the

Maclaurin chaplain at Auckland University, he had sexually assaulted seventeen- and eighteen-year-old students who were either being counselled by him or who were under his leadership within the Student Christian Movement. One of these women had later moved to Christchurch, and although she had not given him her address, R must have gone to some lengths to acquire it; for when he came to Christchurch to be interviewed for the position of principal, which he subsequently obtained, he had arrived at her door unexpectedly and sexually assaulted her.

One morning I read in the newspaper that R's office had burnt out. When I went to see him three weeks later, nothing had been done to erase the effects of the fire. The curtains had been deliberately set alight in three different places, and many of his books and papers had been destroyed. On the wall, in pink pen, someone had written words insulting him and his sexual proclivities. He sat huddled in a chair amidst the chaos. I looked closely at the writing and remarked that it looked as though it had been women who had trashed his office because of the pink pen and the style of writing. He replied that it was quite probable, since they had used the women's toilets. However, he said that he had told the board of governors that it was probably the revenge of a former student about whom he had given a report in court. The board had accepted his explanation and no investigation was carried out. He said that he was planning to build a larger office.

Later, Bishop M asked my vicar if I had been the arsonist. He came round to ask me if I had caused the fire. I was incensed that the bishop suspected me.

What we could not understand was why so many women had kept their liaisons with him secret. Why had no-one gone to the church authorities before now and reported his sexual activities? We were mystified. My only answer to that question is that the women felt the same way as I did—helpless, overwhelmed and powerless under the charisma of a senior churchman. He launched himself sexually at carefully selected women who were vulnerable in one way or another, and then feigned exhaustion and helplessness. He told the women how much he loved them and they believed him. Because they were overwhelmed by his helplessness and exhaustion and his pretence that he was indeed important, they felt privileged that they had been chosen to be loved by him and they gave him everything they had in the way of emotional support, sex, whatever. Whatever he wanted, they gave it to him. Most of all they protected him. Some women still believed that he really did love them. He, in turn, ruthlessly used their energy for himself. These women believed that they were doing it for God and the church but in reality he bent it and twisted it so that it turned out to be for him. He was very subtle, very cunning and very clever. We worked out that he had sexual relations with at least four women over the same time period, maybe more. No wonder he was exhausted. No wonder he would not call a woman by her name—there was a good chance he might have got it wrong.

Suddenly, without warning and without explanation, he told me that he had withdrawn from being my supervisor. He proffered no explanation even though I asked him why, but others informed me that he had withdrawn because he was not getting paid to train me. I found this rather odd since he was already being paid a good salary by the college and he did not get remuneration for any other church work that he did. It was ironic, too, in that I was training for non-stipendiary ministry at my own expense, without his help, and that I had earlier requested a change of supervisor, which had been refused. I was deeply afraid of what was happening behind the scenes. What had he said about me to the committee of examining chaplains? What awful game was he playing now? I had no idea what was going on and I did not dare ask. A short time later, a woman priest who was also a bishop's examining chaplain rang me to say that she had forgotten that she had been appointed as my second spiritual director, but that she would take up that role forthwith.

I felt affronted by the issue of money. He was well paid, his wife was a teacher, and there did not seem to be a shortage of money in the family. I did not believe that money was the real issue. I was angry that he was able to step out of his supervisory role when he wanted to, but I was not able to change supervisors when I wanted to. To me that indicated a lack of respect and a betrayal of trust. On the one hand I was relieved, but on the other I felt suspicious.

Although he was no longer my supervisor R continued to demand my time. When he decided to look for a house in the country he came to me for help. I noted that he had access to me when he wanted but that this was no longer reciprocal. He wanted to buy an old abandoned church somewhere in Canterbury but found instead a derelict pottery factory in a small country village, which had not been used for at least twenty years. Parts of it were rotten and it was entirely covered over with vines. The whole ruin appeared to me to be profoundly symbolic of his inner self and I hoped that he might restore himself at the same time as he restored the old factory. It was on a large section overlooking the domain, which was planted out with old, beautiful trees. He had longings to be a builder and a potter so it all seemed to fit.

Then he started to wonder whether he had enough money. The asking price was ludicrously cheap, and he was wealthy by most people's standards. This incident occurred not long after he had withdrawn from the position of my supervisor, ostensibly on account of the fact that he was not getting paid. Was he asking me for money? Because conversation with him consisted of obtuse hints rather than direct conversation, it was always left to me to figure out what it was he was really saying. I had continued to be angry about the money issue, and when I was confronted with what I believed to be his subtle demands for money I was thrown into confusion yet again. I asked him directly if he wanted me to give him money for the house. His response was neither yes nor no, but if I gave him the money then he would accept it. It was thrown back on me. I had very little money of my own and I was running my own household on a shoestring budget. Money was the one thing I did not have to give. My time and my energy were the only things that I could offer to people. The burden of my inner conflict over this matter was so strong that I thought that the only way I could relieve myself from my mental anguish and indignation was to give him some money. This is how I rationalised it. First of all it would be in lieu of payment for his supervision of me. Second, I hoped that restoring the pottery would engage his time and energy so fully that he would not continue to bother me. And third, at my lowest level of reasoning, I wanted to put him to the test. He was not beyond sexual assault or rape, he was not beyond any acts of indecency, he had no conscience, no boundaries, and no feelings for any other person except artificial feelings that were born from deceit and the desire for self-gratification. Would he also accept money? It was like the final test.

I posted him a cheque. I had no idea whether or not he had received it, and when I asked him if he had received it, he said that he had. He did not say thank you.

I had hoped the house would keep him occupied. But he kept coming back. He wanted to know a plumber. I introduced him to a plumber. He wanted to know a builder. I introduced him to a builder. He engaged these local trades people to do basic repairs on the house. Some time later I discovered that he had been extremely difficult to work for and he had not paid his bills. I was ashamed that I had introduced him to these fine people, who were my personal friends. In the end, no-one would work for him. Even when I asked our farm worker to take a tractor with a scoop to push down the high broom that covered the section at the back of the house, R did not say thank you. Instead of offering thanks, he complained about the mess that had been made and that he would have to clean up. He was impossible. He was the scorpion that kept biting.

Sometime later I read in the church newsletter that my peers were being ordained as deacons and I was not included in the list. I made an appointment with R to demand an explanation for my exclusion. He tried to tell me that I was not ready for ordination. I informed him that I was more than ready to be ordained deacon and that I had already been waiting for four-and-a-half years. On my insistence, an ordination service was arranged to take place in my local church, where I was to be made a deacon. As a matter of courtesy I invited him to preach, but he refused and did not attend the service.

After ordination came post-ordination training, known as POT and affectionately referred to as 'Potty'—potty training for priestlings! Once again there was controversy and dissension. R was in charge of POT. He told me that I did not need to attend because I was non-stipendiary. However, since other non-stipendiary deacons and priests were attending POT, I was unable to discern why my attendance was not compulsory in the same way that it was for the others. Post-ordination training was part of the contract with my vicar, the vestry and myself. I was suspicious about R's motives so I took the matter up with the vicar-general, who could not understand the reason for my exclusion from POT. He took the matter up with R and then wrote to me saying that R was keen for me to attend. The vicar-general must have thought I was a bit odd! In a further conversation I had with R on this matter, he said that I could attend POT but that I may not attend the annual barbecue held at the principal's lodge in case his wife saw me. I was not aware that his wife needed protection from me. I was bewildered and insulted by his conditions for my attendance at POT. R then told me it was politically expedient that I attend POT to the extent that my absence was embarrassing.

Services for those attending POT were held in the college chapel. We took it in turns to lead the services and to preach. When it came to my turn, R led me into the downstairs vestry to robe for the service. He selected an alb for me and spent a long time sorting through the stoles to find a suitable one. I was on his territory and I allowed this to happen. When he put the stole around my neck, he stroked my breasts. He fell to his knees in front of me and wrapped his arms around me and laid his head against my stomach. It was not a good preparation to lead a service before my peers. I was flustered and angry that once again he had taken advantage of me in a situation that demanded my full concentration.

✣

My ordination to priesthood took place in the Christchurch Cathedral in 1989. It was a personal goal, one that I had undertaken to achieve on behalf of the people of my community. I had resolved that I would not reveal anything officially until after my ordination, as I thought that the church would be more inclined to believe the stories of ordained women who had proven their faith and were willing to work for the health and well-being of the church.

In August of that same year, the ordained women in the Anglican Church of New Zealand decided to hold their first conference. It was a wonderful coming together of all of the ordained women in New Zealand to celebrate twelve years of women's ordination. I was asked to be on the organising committee, but I was unable to help since my oldest daughter was sitting her first state exam and I felt that this was a priority.

The programme included a workshop on sexual harassment. The women's network had deliberately added this workshop to the conference in order to initiate a conversation about a problem we knew existed within the structures of the church, but which had not been talked about publicly. I was not able to be present, since I had to go home to take my daughters to the Springston Trophy riding event held in Waimate. To our surprise, nine women attended that workshop, and these nine women pledged confidentiality. The content of the conversation was to be kept secret among the members of the group because the women were afraid of the consequences to their careers in the church. Perhaps they too felt that they had to protect the men who had sexually harassed them. Whatever the reason, the decision to keep confidentiality clearly indicated the secrecy and fear that surrounded the subject of sexuality in the church at that time. It was also abundantly clear that, whatever the reason for the secrecy, no-one was going to divulge what happened in the workshop. The problem still had the potential to remain hidden.

There were fourteen recommendations from the Ordained Women's Conference. These included recommendations on the selection and assessment of women for ordination, justice issues, the continuation of barriers against women's ordination, and sexual harassment in the church. The fourth recommendation was addressed to bishops, standing committees, St John's College and Knox College. It read:

> We have discovered some dynamics of church life which create an environment in which sexual harassment may occur; e.g., robing, travelling, meeting alone, one-to-one contact with men in colleague and pastoral situations. We acknowledge the reality that there may be jealousy from the vicar's wife, the church can include and attract people with difficulties with their sexuality, the nature of the work makes us vulnerable. Sexual harassment in the church can include: sexual jokes, language, people in power positions blocking, inappropriate touching, invasion of space, requests for sex, innuendoes, corporate harassment, e.g. synod. What can we do? Talk about it. Follow hunches. Physically move. Be ready to be honest—practice strategies. Teaching and modelling behaviour. Don't give up. Carry on. Seek support. Work on your self-esteem. Teach about healthy sexuality. Actively develop healthy relationships with clergy and lay leaders' wives.

At the end of the conference, an interviewer on National Radio interviewed one of the organisers of the conference and honed in on the need for a sexual harassment workshop. He asked her if sexual harassment in the church was a problem. She replied that it was. He pushed her further and asked if the problem was with laymen or with clergymen. She replied that both were implicated in inappropriate behaviour. He then asked her again, in an astonished tone, if clergymen sexually harassed women in the church. Once again, she replied in the affirmative. Again he pushed her, wanting to know what form the harassment took and offered the term 'groping' to assist her with her explanation. She declined to comment further. This was the first public revelation of the problem of sexual harassment and abuse by male clergy. It was a milestone.

It also caused a storm. Later that day, this conference organiser told me that she had given the *Dominion* my name and telephone number and said that I could expect a call from a reporter. My own position was unique because I knew about the sexual harassment but, because I had not been at the workshop, I had not pledged confidentiality to the group. Therefore I was the only one who was free to talk to the press. I was in a dilemma. The full burden of public revelation fell on my shoulders. I knew that if I took this single opportunity to speak out, my vocation as a priest would be in jeopardy. I also knew that if I did not take it, other women would still be at risk, and I knew I could not live with this on my conscience. When it came down to the final weighing up, I decided that part of my ministry to other women was to protect them from the dangers that lurked within the very institution that claimed to be a safe haven and a refuge.

My duty was clear. It was not about self-protection but about a syndrome of abuse that had affected not just me but many other women. When the reporter from the *Dominion* rang I was ready to talk. However, it was with some agony that I revealed details about my personal journey towards priesthood. First of all, in the dialogue, I requested anonymity for the sake of my family.

On 7 September 1989 the newspaper ran the article on page one. It was a good article and covered the territory well.

It did not take long for the church hierarchy to track me down. There were not many women priests around with four children. I was sitting down to an evening meal with my family when Bishop M rang. He had just stepped off the plane from an overseas excursion and, as well as being tired, he was extremely angry. He demanded to know why I had not gone to him to talk about the problem. I told him that I did not have enough confidence in him to deal with the problem and that he would have swept it under the carpet and got rid of me. He asked me if I would like to speak to the archbishop. I replied that I would be delighted to speak with the archbishop if he wanted to speak with me. But I was nervous about talking to the archbishop, in spite of my bravado. However nervous I was though, I did not expect such an outright attack from the leader of the church. I was taken aback by his line of questioning. He informed me that I was completely at fault and blamed me, casting aspersions about my moral character. He said that R was a victim. I wondered where his allegiances lay. They certainly did not lie with me and other women who might be in danger. His first allegiance seemed to be to R and the church.

TWO

The struggle to be heard

The news media were naturally extremely interested in the issue. The archbishop was interviewed in *The Press* (7 Sept 1989, p.6) and said that male priests were 'red-blooded males' just like every other man and that 'it took two to tango'. The women were breathless with incredulity and told the archbishop so. At every other interview with the press he had to take a minder with him to ensure that he did not make such inflammatory and outrageous remarks again. Sandra Coney took up the issue in the *Dominion Sunday Times* (24 Sept 1989, p. 8) where she informed the general public of New Zealand that sexual harassment is not new, only talking about it is:

> One of the Anglican priests said she had been so upset by harassment from male clergy during her training she thought of abandoning her career in the church. That is of course precisely what the men want. Sexual harassment, as feminists have long pointed out, is a method of social control, like all other forms of male violence. Violence preserves power, by intimidating individual women and serving notice on their sex of what they too risk. It is a reminder of our vulnerability and of the randomness of male violence...
>
> The Anglican priest said male priests would always stick together. Clergywomen in New Zealand were afraid to speak because it might be used by overseas churches to keep 'trouble-making' women out...Sexual harassment is a means of keeping women down and out. In male-intensive industries it ensures sexual exclusivity...Sexual harassers are terrorists for their sex. Or 'ordinary red blooded males like anywhere else' as Archbishop D, head of the Anglicans said. Take your pick.

The bishop of Christchurch was interviewed in *The Press* (9 Sept 1989, p.4). The article was headed 'Diocese to look into harassment'. Bishop M said that 'sexual harassment merely reflected New Zealand society, which generally has not dealt very well with sexuality'. He was reported as saying that the Christchurch Diocese would most probably consider sexual harassment along with the other twenty recommendations from the conference. He said that the church would take it seriously.

The church did not take the issue seriously. Two weeks went by without any communication from the Diocesan Office or the bishop. It was evident that he hoped it would go away so that he would not have to deal with the matter. My vicar rang the bishop to prod him into action and invited him to come and see me. He would not come but in his place sent out the dean of the Christchurch Cathedral in his position as vicar-general. As I told my full story to him I shook uncontrollably, racked with feelings of anxiety, guilt and betrayal. The dean listened very carefully. He told me that if I wanted to make a written formal complaint, it would ensure that the church would follow the correct procedure for this sort of complaint. Our worst suspicions were confirmed, which were that the bishop would not even consider the matter until formal complaints in writing were sent to him.

My friend from the West Coast, the Reverend Patricia Allan, who was a great ally and supporter, met the dean immediately after this meeting and found him in a state of shock. Later, my vicar telephoned Patricia and asked her to invite the other women that we knew of who had been sexually abused by R to make written complaints and send them to the bishop, although he said that my case would stand on its own without the support of the other complaints. Accordingly, I received a letter from Patricia. She, together with the Reverend Hilary Barlow, had met with the vicar-general to discuss the sexual harassment issues and possible ongoing procedures. The letter expressed the vicar-general's concern that a complaint be put in writing so that the bishop could proceed according to the canons and statutes of the church. Patricia noted in this letter her expectation that three commissioners would be appointed to establish whether or not there was a case to be answered. She wrote:

> Whilst her harassment has been extreme and is probably sufficient to establish a *prima facie* case, I believe that it is important that other women at this time speak up about this unwanted behaviour. Her vicar has asked me if I would get a letter drafted with legal assistance and seek to gain the signatures of other women who would if necessary be willing to give evidence. My legal advisor, the chancellor of another diocese, has pointed out that because the accusations of harassment by this man are now fairly widespread it is only fair to him and to the bishop that his case be properly heard. This is scary for all of us but I am personally willing to hang in until the whole thing is resolved for the sake of the ongoing health of the church. If you feel able to sign this letter would you please do so and send it directly to the bishop. You have no need to tell me whether or not you have done so. Of course, if you wanted to modify it in any way that would be perfectly alright.

The dean had written a report of my story from memory. I went to see him to thank him for listening to me and to check that what he had written was accurate. It was not completely accurate, and he had left portions of the story out. When I told him so, he replied that he was so disgusted that his fingers could barely touch the keys of his typewriter and that he could not bring himself to write down the worst bits. I was worried about this report. The dean had filed it as 'extremely confidential', but it seemed to me there was too much confidentiality in these situations. Confidentiality enabled the aggrieved party to discuss a serious issue freely. On the other hand it meant that the issue could never be dealt with fully out in the open. We had expected the dean to be an advocate, not a counsellor. We expected him to share the information with other clergy in the hierarchy. Because we did not realise that it had gone no further than the dean, we were confused and bewildered by the seeming lack of information, which resulted in spite and malice. Divisions and schisms happened between people. Rumours began, and so did the abusive telephone calls. One woman priest rang to denounce me and told me that I had shot myself in the foot—meaning, I presume, that I had damaged only myself and no-one else.

We were shocked that week when the bishop announced his resignation. It was rumoured that he had not been well and had been considering retirement. We felt betrayed and abandoned at a time of great crisis. He had been elected as bishop because of his ability to offer pastoral care to his clergy. Now, when his skills were most needed, he was unable to offer them. Although he had announced his retirement, he declared that he would not vacate his seat for six months in order to give the synod time to appoint a new bishop. Throughout these six months his heart was not in it. He was unable to guide us through these troubled waters of conflict, grief, affliction and division.

My vicar decided that if the bishop could not come out to the country, then we would go to see him in the bishop's house. Once again the bishop had to be nudged into action. This was not a successful interview. I did not want to go, for I knew with an unwavering clarity that the bishop regarded me as a 'sinner' for whom there was no redemption. Why? Because I had 'told' on the men. I was very angry and upset, and was no longer willing to be part of a church that treated fifty per cent of its members, those who were women, with such appalling inhumanity and injustice, and where sexual violation and abuse were condoned and covered up. Accordingly, I put my Licence to Officiate as Deacon and my Licence to Officiate as Priest in my bag, with the intention of handing them over to the bishop as a stand against injustice. I had not warned my vicar of my intention, so it took him by surprise when I handed them over to the bishop. I wanted to let the bishop know just how serious an issue this was and that if he was not going to deal with it through church processes then I wanted to be free to go to secular justice services. It was not only my licences I was giving up. I was giving up my priesthood, six hard years of training. The bishop took my licences and put them away in his desk. He said that he would keep them until the time came to give them back. By his acceptance of these documents I was suspended. Two other things happened at this interview. He said that the church would pay for one counselling session for me with a counsellor of his choice. He also advised me not to sit any exams that year. Then he blessed me and we left.

I felt indignant that he had advised me not to complete my study. From the very beginning he had thought my study a waste of time and had taken active steps to discourage it. This was his final effort to prevent my academic endeavour. I decided against his advice not to sit my exams—once again I was forced to disobey the bishop's commands. It was my final year for both an LTh. and BD. I had done all the work for eight papers and it was now September. There did not seem much point in delaying by another year. It was evident that the bishop did not approve of educated women. Or perhaps he thought I was suffering a nervous collapse from overwork and studying and needed to take a break.

For the next six weeks I went to a friend's house each day to study. I did not feel safe being at home alone during the day. We did not know how R would react to what was going on, but we were all afraid that something violent might occur.

✣

The churchwomen had begun to work hard producing a flurry of correspondence that sought ways to work through the issues on sexual harassment. They were impelled by strong feelings about injustice and lack of fair play. The Reverend Patricia Allan took a lead role, and continued to do so throughout her short-lived career in the Anglican Church. She was a strong advocate for the creation of national guidelines for dealing with sexual harassment and abuse in the church. The canons provided a two-year clause for complaints of this nature; Patricia did not feel this was enough time, since she knew from her own experience as a priest and counsellor that it would take people years to have the courage to speak out about their abuse. She said in a letter to the women's network:

> I fear that if each diocese is left to appoint its own women to be pastorally responsible for individual complaints then these women could be picked off by the people in power. This has already happened to me and is not comfortable. Thus, I think a representative provincial group would be more appropriate and effective. If this group was not to be subjected to sabotage then it would need to work within clearly laid down and accepted guidelines.
>
> At present I am also concerned that there is a confusion between justice and mercy, sin and sickness and that the scales are coming down much more in favour of the abuser than his victims...My question now is Where do we go from here? I have some energy to address these issues but am not at all clear on procedure. It seems to me that this would be the kind of agenda for the representative women's group. We must use the generated energy wisely and well. In the last few days I have come to believe that R must be stripped completely. What he has done is a scandal to the Gospel. No longer am I satisfied with social work liberation!

The Reverend Janet Crawford wrote to Patricia on 26 October 1989, saying she was determined that the eventual outcome should be positive. She suggested that the whole issue should be part of the agenda for the then Provincial Board of Ministry (PBM) sub-committee, which was to be set up on the recommendation from the Ordained Women's Conference. The problem with this procedure was the time it would take to set up the sub-committee. She suggested that as an interim measure the PBM be asked to set up a working group on sexual harassment. The main objective of this working group would be to get material out for discussion and revision as soon as possible in the hope of getting something in for General Synod in 1990.

Janet also sent out the following circular letter, on 27 October 1989:

> Dear Friends
>
> I have learned that Waiapu and Wellington dioceses have set up groups to work on guidelines on sexual harassment. It does seem important that we keep one another informed—presumably that information could have been very helpful for Pat and the other Christchurch women. I suggest that until we have some sort of provincial group we keep in touch by circulating information, news, etc, through members of the original planning group. We really need the support that we can give to women throughout the province and to continue the networking that was begun at the conference. Please let's do our best to build on what has been begun, in this case by sharing what is happening.

At the same time that the women were strongly motivated to do something, R was allowed free rein in his office. The board of governors had given him a lawyer to help him with the processes. He had free access to the college telephone and used this significant resource to gather up his friends and colleagues to defend him. He vilified the women, claiming that we had thrown ourselves at him. We all knew better.

To put things on a more formal basis, according to the original suggestion of the dean, in September 1989 four brave but nervous women priests submitted formal written complaints to the bishop following the procedure laid down by the church canons. We had faith in the process, even though we could not foresee the future and were ill-prepared for this pioneering journey for the church. The complaints read as follows:

> We, being clergy, officials or members of the church of the Province of New Zealand, wish to bring a complaint against R, a priest of the Diocese of Christchurch in relation to Title D Canon 11 5.4 (c) of the Canons of the Province of New Zealand.
>
> The complaint is one of sexual harassment, defined as 'unwanted imposition of sexual behaviour in a context of unequal power' and committed in respect to the undersigned complainant.
>
> We respectfully request that you promptly and appropriately investigate this complaint.

I felt uneasy about signing the complaint form. Even though I knew that his sexual behaviour was sick and perverted, he had also been my mentor and guide, my pastoral and liturgical trainer. I felt ambivalent about it to the extent that I felt that I was betraying him. I had not been able to help him and he needed help. This was not the way to go about it, but there was no other way for him to get the sort of help that he desperately needed. I knew something had to be done to stop his wanton destruction of women. I signed not in a blind fury, although that was there too, but out of a deep and terrible sadness for a talented man who was unable to control his own sexuality. In a sense I felt that I was also betraying God and myself.

While these complaints were being filed, I was called in to see my doctor on the pretext that she needed to talk to me. By that time I could scarcely walk because of the stress and the anguish of the whole business. She wrote out a medical certificate requesting that I cease official duties for up to three months. On the certificate, which was sent to the bishop, she wrote that she had been involved with me over the years in connection with the problem and she believed the whole issue to be so important that it was essential the matter be set aside until such a time as she considered that I was well enough to deal with it. However, I was not the only complainant so the process was not inhibited by my stress.

Once we had submitted our complaints, we waited. There was nothing; no visible action, no consultation with the women. Nothing at all. On the 20 October 1989, a full month after our complaints had been submitted, Bishop M wrote to inform us that, while he took seriously any allegations of sexual harassment or misconduct, 'the complaints about the Reverend Canon R, although unspecific in some cases and unsubstantiated in others, have been investigated'. He also said that 'the evidence which has been furnished does not lie within the past two years as is required by General Synod regulations and therefore a formal commission cannot be set up under the canons (see Title D Canon II).'

We were shocked on two counts. The reference to unspecific and unsubstantiated complaints was ridiculous. None of us had been asked by the bishop what our evidence was. I wondered what had happened to the report that the dean had written after he had come to see me in the place of the bishop. I knew that report outlined very specific evidence, although important information had been excluded because of his own revulsion. I also knew that he had labelled that report 'extremely confidential'. I began to suspect that he had not shared his report with anybody else, for how else could the bishop claim that our complaints were not substantiated?

The second issue that he outlined was that a formal commission could not be set up to hear the complaints because the sexual harassment or misconduct had not occurred within the last two years. The bishop had asked only two out of the four women when the behaviour had occurred. He had deliberately not asked the two of us for whom the misconduct had occurred during the last two years. And neither would he listen to us when we explained to him that he had asked only two of the complainants and had in fact taken the experience of the two to include all four. He had an opportunity at this point to redress his neglect and to institute the proper proceedings as they were laid down in the canons. But he chose not to do this. We were outraged. It was clear that the bishop was attempting to put barriers up deliberately so that the complaints would be invalidated. In his letter he continued as follows:

> The Reverend Canon R has been formally admonished and warned and has had seniority removed: He was not permitted to stand for General Synod, he is no longer an examining chaplain, he is no longer involved in any way with post-ordination training, he has been replaced on the Provincial Board of Ministry and on Theological Education by Extension. There will not be any situation in which he will supervise women alone. He has commenced regular therapy and will continue in therapy to ensure that attitudes are carefully monitored. He is required to be in supervision. He has been removed from training roles except in group situations in a limited role when called in by someone else.

The truth was that although R had been removed from his positions of seniority, he had not had his licence to function as a priest removed. This meant that he would still have access to women in his position as priest. Moreover, on the grounds that the church did not employ R, the bishop had abdicated from all responsibility of solving or resolving the complaints. The bishop informed us that the board of governors now had the responsibility of considering R's position as the principal of the college and that the board would communicate separately with us. If we wanted to take the matter further he told us that we should make another formal complaint to his employers, the college board of governors.

This was an interesting twist to events. Pilate was washing his hands. I began to understand the meaning of 'stonewalling'. Even though the diocese had appointed R to so many of its most pivotal and vital activities, at the final count they refused to take responsibility for his behaviour towards the very people that he had been appointed to care for. The church leaders abdicated from responsibility and devolved it to the givers of his salary, who were now seen to be the guardians of his moral behaviour. It was not the moral power of the church that came to be at stake, but money. Although the board of governors paid him a salary to be principal of the college with male university students under his care, it was not to these that his abusive behaviour was directed. He sexually exploited the people whom the church entrusted to his care—for selection, for training and for teaching—and for this role he was *not* paid. The other anomaly that became apparent was that the college was under the auspices of the Anglican Church and the bishop was the chairman of the board of governors. The college was not autonomous but was ruled by the church. The church had side-stepped the whole affair on the grounds of money.

It was a clever diversionary tactic. It succeeded. It caused confusion, anger and fear in the hearts of the women who had submitted their complaints to the bishop in the belief that the church would provide processes to deal with a difficult issue. We were confused as to the reason why we had been asked to submit our complaints again. We were angry that the church had betrayed us into the hands of the board. We were fearful because the board was constituted of men who were lawyers, barristers and judges and who governed a traditional, conservative, male, church-based university hall. We knew instinctively that they would not take our complaints seriously. We began to understand the significance of the deep, underlying patriarchal nature of the church, which would always stand in judgement against women. We were condemned to be at fault before we even began.

✣

The board of governors of the college sent a letter to me care of my vicar, not to my home address. The letter quoted a resolution made at their meeting on 19 October:

> The board notes that the warden in his capacity as bishop of Christchurch has received a number of allegations against the principal which may reflect on the principal's fitness to continue to hold the position of principal of the college, and that the persons concerned be asked to make a formal complaint to the board should they wish to do so.

The sub-warden outlined the procedure clearly. If a formal complaint is received, the board or a sub-committee of the board will set a date to hear the complaint in full and will give Canon R the opportunity to answer that complaint. A suitably qualified person will be appointed to hear the complaint and communicate his finding to the board. The board will then act upon those findings.

We began again. The first complaint had been hard enough to make. The second was even harder. The submission was now a legal complaint to a secular body that did not claim to have the compassion of Christ but instead the fury of the law. We felt in great danger. We were commanded to submit our complaints to the board's solicitor by 5pm on 6 November 1989. We requested an extension until 20 November so that we could consider our position. The implication of the letter was that if we did not comply with this then our complaints would be invalid. There was also a thinly veiled threat in the letter with regard to the board acting on the findings of the suitably qualified man who would control the proceedings. We were well aware that this was not a court of law but a kangaroo court set up by the board to defend their principal. It was highly likely we could be sued for libel. In full knowledge of the dangers we faced, we submitted our complaints on 20 November for consideration by the board on 4 December.

We were made strong by the pathetic inability of the diocese to confront this issue. We had been denied our rightful access to proper processes. The diocese had not only let us down, it had let itself down. Four frail and frightened women, girded only with their vulnerability and an insistence and persistence for justice, clambered over the ruins of the church to face the world of secular injustice. We were prepared for anything that might befall us. We were even prepared to go to prison if that was what it took to see that justice was done. We were stirred to our very souls.

We were poor in terms of resources. We had no money to pay for legal advice against a powerful and wealthy board committed to the preservation and protection of a male-dominated institution with infinite resources at its disposal. On the other hand the board had given R free access to its own solicitor and to all the resources of his office at the college. R used all his powers of manipulation and coercion to get everyone from the archbishop down on his side. We knew that this was going to be hard.

It took even more energy to submit our second complaint to the board of governors. We became even more determined to ensure that this matter be heard. My determination was so strong that I drove for an hour into Christchurch to deliver my complaint to the office of the board's solicitor, insisted that my complaint be faxed through immediately to the secretary of the board and waited until the indication came through that it had been received. I was not willing to entrust a letter to the postal system, where it could get lost or the recipient could say that it had not been received. I had lost trust in institutions, systems, processes and men.

We women stood close together, strongly supported by other women in the church community who understood our struggle for justice, who prayed with us and for us. We were all strengthened by prayer and prepared to fight for justice. We knew the odds were against us. We were all afraid, even with this immense and wonderful support. We needed someone to advise us how to act and considered the options closely. The possibility that the board or R could sue us for libel was strong. Some amongst us thought that, as a point of principle, we should have a woman lawyer to represent us. Others of us believed that a man would be heard better by other men. In the meantime we heard nothing. Four intelligent, well-educated and professional women who were priests of the church and who had dared to complain about sexual harassment and abuse of power were ignored.

In desperation I rang a close friend, N, who was a barrister. He was perceptive and got to the heart of the matter quickly. He was extremely concerned about our situation, and was sharp, crisp, clear and analytical. He acted immediately. He arranged for me to see a solicitor. He reserved a criminal barrister to represent me in court. Finally, he rang the secretary of the board of governors of the college to inform him of the actions that he had undertaken on our behalf.

The result of my barrister friend's action in ringing the secretary of the board was extraordinary. It appeared that the board had not taken our complaints seriously and had had no intention of doing anything with them. Now, when they saw that we were in deadly earnest and would take them to court if they did not do something, their hand was forced. Either they could sue us for libel, which would give them bad publicity, or they could dismiss R, or force his resignation.

N's advice to me as a friend was that the court process was a harrowing experience. Any woman who brought a case to court against a man for sexual misdemeanours was certain to be profoundly humiliated and exposed. He told me that from his experience, whatever the outcome of the case, the woman's marriage would inevitably fall apart and she would be ostracised from her family, friends and community. I gave careful thought to his advice. Of course the temptation was there to inform the world who was right and who was wrong in this matter, but for the sake of survival it was better left. But I was shocked at his advice. The church hierarchy had refused justice. And now the realm of secular law made it difficult for women to take their complaints to court and acted to humiliate women before it would mete out justice. It felt as though we had touched the rawest nerve of the human community. The determination of men to preserve their own power over women was deep-seated in every institution. There were some supporters who urged me to file a complaint with the police and have the matter taken to court in order to prove publicly that R was guilty. The diocese was not prepared to take any action against him because they believed that the women were wrong; the board would not acknowledge that his behaviour was inappropriate; and so the matter was left in the hands of a small group of women who knew that there was a problem but had no institutional support and no money to push for justice. Perhaps we should have taken the matter to court. It would have resolved it one way or another.

✣

Each woman complainant received a letter, dated 5 December, from the secretary of the board of governors of the college, announcing that the board had received and accepted the resignation of Canon R, effective from 28 February 1990. The letter added 'the board is accordingly not now in the position to pursue the matters raised in the correspondence between us'.

Several members of the board of governors approached me. One advised me to disappear for a few years. Another asked me what was wrong with exposing oneself in public. Another, who was the vicar's warden in my home parish, did not support the women and, although the information was confidential, he told his wife, who talked about it freely with her friends. This was not helpful.

Had we complained so that R would resign? R was gone—gone from the college and gone from the diocese. Was that what we had wanted? Several of our worries were salved by this result. The women students entering the college for the first time would be protected from his sexually predatory behaviour. So would the churchwomen who came into the college for theological education, training and course work. This in itself was good.

However, there were two factors that gave us further concern. The first was the knowledge that R had been allowed to resign from his position as principal. The reason for his resignation was set aside as the board farewelled him at a party given in his honour and gave him what was rumoured to be a $60,000 golden handshake—a year's salary. We heard that the speechmaker at the farewell party publicly apologised to R for the victimisation and false accusations from which he had suffered at the hands of the women. A prominent woman minister in the Methodist Church had written him a reference, even though she must have heard about the complaints against him, and he had immediately obtained employment as provost of a new college in Palmerston North, where young Asian students came to learn English as a second language. We were concerned that the problem had not gone away. It had merely been removed from our attention. What about those other women out there to whom he could still be a danger? The second factor that we did not anticipate was that the board of governors of the college shrugged off its church mantle and refused to allow any more church activities to take place on the premises. There was to be no more theological education, training or worship. The board was split into two parts: one to govern the university hostel, the other to make alternative provisions for theological education.

The church community within the diocese and outside it was alive with gossip, rumours and innuendoes. In order to quell these rumours, the bishop was persuaded to write a memo to all clergy outlining the events that had taken place. It was insisted that the women be recognised and thanked for their courage in confronting such behaviour. On 8 December 1989 a confidential trial text was put out for discussion only, with no claim to be official. It was entitled 'Memo Re Diocesan Procedures for Hearing Charges of Sexual Immorality and Harassment'. It had been put together by an *ad hoc* committee of people who supported R and felt that he had been treated badly by the women. We felt that it was another attempt by the bishop to make light of the matter by producing a document just to make people happy. The text read:

> **On the norms of sexual behaviour:**
> Because a variety of different, even conflicting, views on issues of sexual morality exist in the Anglican Church, the larger Christian community and the society at large, the bishop states the following policy and procedure as applicable to this diocese.
>
> Clergy and staff of the diocese are expected to lead a life which is a wholesome example to all people. Such a life includes all the positive aspects of sexuality but quite clearly excludes the following: sexual intercourse outside the bonds of marriage, adulterous relationships and the practice of homosexuality or sexual harassment. The proper Christian approach to cases of sexual immorality, as to all immorality, should be pastoral, not legalistic and merely condemnatory.
>
> **Sexual Harassment:**
> If you think you are being sexually harassed, talk to someone you trust. It is important to talk it over and get support. This support might come from someone in your family, a friend or someone with whom you work.
>
> Approach the harasser, alone or with someone else. Tell him/her you don't like his/her behaviour and you want it to stop.

If you still feel under pressure after talking to him/her, you should go at once to the bishop, or the vicar-general if, for canonical reasons, the bishop is unavailable.

The bishop will appoint two clergy, one female and one male, to interview the person making the report. They will then hear the response of the person accused. This series of interviews should happen as soon as possible and in private.

Other clergy or laity aware of rumour must refrain from speculation, in public or private, out of consideration for the families of those involved and for the parishes involved. If they want to talk about the matter they must go directly to the bishop.

The bishop may direct the appropriate archdeacon or some other priest to confront those known to be spreading rumour. Trust in the bishop's pastoral concern is basic to the life of the diocese.

The two clergy interviewers will consult with the bishop on the outcome of their interviews. Except for clearly unavoidable reasons this process from first report to this consultation must not take more than seven days.

The bishop will move to call the two parties concerned together, each with a supporting friend, and the meeting [will be] conducted by a mediator appointed by the bishop. Again, every effort will be made to see that this meeting occurs within seven days.

It is hoped that Christians will be able to resolve the situation in this way to ease the stress on the families of both parties as well as the parties involved.

If a satisfactory conclusion is not reached within this fortnight, it is possible for either party to proceed through the facilities of the Human Rights Commission.

Another text was attached to this memo for discussion:

Sexual Immorality

Matters of the sexual immorality of the clergy should be brought to the attention of the bishop in a written declaration by the accuser and the procedures followed as set forth under Canon II, Title D, section 5 of the church of the Province of New Zealand.

If one knows of sexual immorality on the part of a clergy person it is in order to bring this knowledge to her/his attention with the object of having it cease and/or of offering help. It is also the responsibility of anyone with such knowledge to communicate this to the bishop.

When such a case comes to the attention of the bishop s/he should appoint someone to oversee or to manage the situation or undertake the task herself/himself. Part of this task is to see that those concerned including the parish are cared for and helped in a creative way to come to terms with the situation.

No response will be made unless charges or allegations are given in writing.

The matter should be dealt with concisely and without delay.

It should be possible to give the clergy person and the parish a space to deal with the situation. The vicar should be rested and a locum appointed.

Other clergy or laity aware of rumour must refrain from speculation, in public or in private, out of consideration for the families of those involved and for the parishes involved. If they want to talk about the matter they must go directly to the bishop.

Standing Committee should be asked to set up a fund which may be used to pay people whose lives are in difficulty for whatever reason. This would allow freedom of those responding to a need to withdraw the licence of the clergy person so that s/he may have a break on full stipend.

These documents were offered to the clergy for discussion. They were clearly off-target for the situation under discussion, and various points were raised that had absolutely nothing to do with the present situation under review. The Reverend John Shallcrass, Lecturer in Theology and New Testament at the college, took up advocacy on our account and replied in writing with a well-thought-out critique of both texts. The letter shows clearly how the issues of sexual harassment began to be intellectually wrestled with in order to gain a full understanding.

Reverend Shallcrass wondered why the issue of sexual morality was introduced in a context of sexual harassment:

> **(a)** It confuses two related but clearly distinct categories. While sexual harassment presents as a sexual issue with sexual implications, it is fundamentally an issue of power rather than sex, an issue of someone having been given power over someone else and abusing the responsibility to behave for their good rather than take advantage. It would seem to me that classifying sexual harassment with issues of sexual morality masks this essential point. It also prevents those having to think about such a matter and deal with it from getting to the real issues. (This is a philosophic point perhaps, but not without practical implications. In the present case, the church's quite proper horror at what has happened sexually has, it seems to us, diverted attention from a serious matter: the question of safeguards in the system against such abuse of power).
>
> **(b)** It allows the impression there are problems of sexual immorality among the clergy [in general] that also need dealing with. Are there? Is there evidence for this? If so, let's have it and deal with it. If not, why raise the possibility of such interpretation? To create the impression there are such problems when, as far as I'm aware, there are not, would be totally unfair to the clergy in general. Speaking personally, I think we clergy who try to behave honourably in sexual matters have suffered enough as a result of

this individual's behaviour; to have the bishop and those close to him allow the impression now that we as a group need watching in matters of general sexual immorality seems grossly unjust.

What we have been dealing with is a specific case of a specific problem. Can we not deal specifically with it, thereby avoiding other and hurtful complications and implications? Whose interests are served by broadening the matter in this way?

Is such a statement needed?

The specific case has been dealt with, the offender has been disciplined, at least to the extent of being removed from his position. This now is known to the clergy and presumably to those in their parishes who have known and been concerned. The bishop has agreed to make a statement that the case of sexual harassment in this diocese has been dealt with and that those who raised the matter should be commended; which ought to give protection to those involved from slander and innuendo. Once this is done, is there need for anything more? As sensible people keep saying, actions speak louder than words. If these actions have been taken, people will draw the obvious conclusion—that the church will listen to those claiming sexual harassment, and will discipline those who harass. Is there need for another statement, especially a statement that shifts the focus away from the real issue?

The real issues for the future?

(a) For the sake of potential victims and those who could have to help them, it would be useful to provide simple guidelines, akin to those worked out by other professional organisations. There are a number available.

(b) The emphasis here, it seems to me, should not be on setting up structures people are expected to use (electing a priest, counsellor, confidant as one's listener/supporter is too personal for that). The emphasis should be things for the victim to think about, and check out, on the way to finding a listener/confidant; from which point the steps by which the matter is taken to the bishop will depend on particular circumstances.

(c) For the sake of working clergy there be directed discussion at Clergy School on the matter of pastoral relations with members of the opposite sex; there could be optional workshops at Clergy School or elsewhere for learning better to understand and deal effectively with such relationships.

Some specific points in the document

As I say, I think we would be better to let the church's action speak at this point. Or, if guidelines must be laid down for dealing with sexual harassment, they should deal just with that, not with issues of sexual morality in general. But as far as the document itself is concerned I have the following concerns:

The term 'sexual morality'

There is a question whether this is appropriate in this particular context. What is at issue here is not, I take it, the church's proclamation of sexual morality as such; but what it does and ought to do, in its general proclamation, life and care for its own and for others. What is at issue is the more specific matter of enforcing sexual discipline. This is a limited thing, reflecting our commitment to sexual morality as such, but restricted to proscribing certain serious and destructive forms of sexual malpractice. This restriction, it seems to me, reflects the church's compassionate realism, that while, as clergy, we can be expected to refrain from acts that directly harm others, none of us inwardly, or in other ways, is without our sexual tensions.

What concerns me is that the use of the term 'sexual morality' where what is at issue is 'proscribing sexual malpractice' could lead to a blurring of this distinction, a blurring that could lead to the kind of moralistic crusading that denies God's compassion on our fallibility.

Those knowing of sexual immorality to contact the bishop

I am extremely concerned at this suggestion. It seems to me to infringe a basic principle of justice, the distinction between the person who reports in as a victim and the person who reports in on hearsay. Surely the invitation to report sexual immorality must be restricted to the victim or the victim's nominee. What has happened to the pastoral and ethical principle that it is the person involved, as the one who really knows, the one for whom the issue matters, who should be listened to? Have the writers of the document not thought this through? If we follow the principle that anyone may report, we invite busybodies, bearers of grudges, the vindictive, the mean-minded to get to work and strut their stuff. And it doesn't take a great deal of historical recollection to see where that kind of thing leads!

General impression of the document

As it stands, the document strikes me as something of a panic reaction. It could be summed up 'When you hear of sexual immorality, go to the bishop. Don't breathe a word to a soul. Go straight to the bishop, and he and his advisors will sort the matter out'.

There is nothing wrong with the principle of putting the matter in the hands of the bishop. There is clearly a need to keep things decently confidential. But to focus simply on these particular principles is to leave the way open to the kind of confusion, unfairness and delay that has so badly marred the present investigation. It would seem to me that other principles ought also to be included, principles such as:

(a) *The principle of protection through separation of roles:* that those assigned to support either party should be restricted to that role; that they should not be involved in any way in advising the bishop on the conduct of the investigation as such.

(b) *The principle of protecting the interests of both parties equally, from the preliminary investigation on.* Not being a lawyer, I can't spell these out, but if the bishop or bishop's nominee is to interview both accuser and accused, to see if there is a *prima facie* case, the rules governing fairness to both parties—allowing them equal knowledge of procedures, allowing them equal chance to respond to each other's allegations and so on—should be enforced.

(c) *The principle, once a* prima facie *case is established, of suspending the accused from office till the issue is resolved:* this is so the parties meet as equals, and the accused is precluded from using the power and status of office unfairly to influence the outcome.

(d) *The principle of a fair minimum release of information to others involved or affected by the issue*—information such as the fact that the case is under investigation, the expected procedure of the investigation, and when an outcome would be expected: This is to allow those involved or affected to deal fairly and cleanly with their own suspicions, and also with those of others concerned who approach them. (Thus the document seems to overlook the fact that the ordinary people, clergy and lay, can be trusted to deal honestly with sensitive information.)

(e) *The principle of gathering information, allegations, etc. thoroughly and systematically, so that all that is relevant comes in, and before judicial proceedings begin.* This is to ensure the bishop has the information from both sides, and complete, so as to ensure appropriate procedures are taken from the outset.

(f) *The principle of distinguishing the administering of justice from the practice of compassion.* This is not to deny the place of compassion. It is to insist that compassion not subvert justice but follow on from it. If justice is not done, one of the parties, *ipso facto*, is unjustly treated. If justice is not done, compassion becomes in effect an offer of cheap grace; and cheap grace has no healing power.

(g) *The principle of making the outcome known, of stating clearly whether there was or was not truth in the allegations made.* This is to lay the matter to rest, vindicating the innocence of the innocent party, indicating to others involved or affected where the truth lies.

And so on. I am not an expert in these areas, but what I have observed of the recent investigation suggests to me that those who wrote the document have been utterly unaware of the difficulty the complainants have had in countering the power of the accused to affect proceedings adversely, because of his position in the hierarchy and the influence it has given him. What the writers fail to recognise is that the dice are institutionally loaded in favour of clergy, particularly those in senior or provincially visible positions. No matter how fair-minded a bishop may be, fair-mindedness is not sufficient in itself to ensure a fair hearing. What is needed is the checks and balances and safeguards of normal legal process, to ensure the bishop gets all the data, gets it early and is free from institutional considerations to act upon it in a fair-minded way. If procedures are to be set up, this too must be recognised.

The Reverend John Shallcrass's analysis of the situation presented us with a clarity that thus far had eluded us. The issues had been deliberately obfuscated so that we had no idea what was happening. One of us said that up until then we had felt as though we were swimming in marshmallow. John's critical analysis of the two documents was thorough, professional and offered fairness to both parties. He was the only person who seemed able to comment on the process thus far, to distinguish between sexual morality and sexual abuse. He opened a door to us and to the church at the same time.

He wrote a second letter to the bishop, which is important to print in full.

Dear Bishop M

For the three or four months this R affair has been in progress, I have been on the point of writing. I have refrained from doing so.

I write now because, his resignation being known, I will no longer be in danger of interfering in something not directly my business.

The reason I am writing is not to express anger, though I confess to being angry—angry for the women involved, angry for myself as a colleague and fellow priest. The reason I am writing is that, as a member of the staff, I have observed the effects of this business. I have observed the effects of the way it has been handled, I have thought often and hard about it. I accept that, as an observer, I have had only a partial view; that those involved will have had to consider matters I am unaware of. But I want you to know that what I have seen has left me puzzled and disillusioned.

For instance, I cannot understand why, when the charges had been laid and found to have substance, the principal was not required to take leave of absence. You may recall that, at about that time, a teacher in the city was accused of being physical with his children and that he was suspended till the charges had been heard. I would have thought the church, certainly on a matter as serious as this, would have been as punctilious. It is not just that the church, having realised the charges were serious, failed to ensure the plaintiff and complainants faced each other on equal footing; though that I would have thought basic to the process. It is that the principal should have been left in possession of the resources of his office, which would allow him to sustain the impression the issue was not serious, to call people to reassure those who were suspicious, to engage the support of those who were sympathetic and to accuse those he had heard were critical. The effect has been to cause suspicion and division among clergy and students, between those who believe the principal to be innocent (or at least not very guilty) and those who believe he is not. I would also mention that allowing the principal to maintain the pretence that things were normal has made the college over recent months a most difficult and unpleasant place for us, and for those of our students who have known the facts or heard the rumours.

A second matter I cannot understand. I cannot understand why it has taken the church as long as it has to deal with what seems such a blatant and destructive abuse of power; the kind of abuse that in other professions, I imagine, would have been dealt with at once. I am told the principal has claimed the women 'threw themselves at him'. I am inclined to believe those who claim this was not so. I would have thought it a principle in supervision that the supervisor, as the one with authority for procedures, had responsibility for ensuring that physical relationships were ruled out—whatever the feelings or actions of the client.

Please do not get me wrong. I am not suggesting this is always easy. I am not suggesting someone who fails should not get the chance to learn the disciplines of handling such matters. What I am suggesting is that where, as appears to be so here, someone persistently refuses or fails to learn the disciplines, persistently allows such relationships to develop, I cannot see how there could possibly be hesitation in removing him. If, as I tend to believe, the issue in this case is not so much an inability to handle transference as persistent and deliberate predation, the imperative for removal would seem to me to have been even stronger. And if, as I understand it to be, it is a matter of pressuring women who had accepted the vulnerability of offering for ordination, ordination to an office where they expected to serve God, the imperative for dealing swiftly, of leaving no doubt at all as to the seriousness of the issue, would seem to me to have been totally undeniable. Do you yourself remember the vulnerable hopefulness, the awed joyfulness of the time when you yourself offered? That a priest of the church could persistently act in ways that corrupted that time for those in his charge is a betrayal I find very very hard to bear with. That the church should have needed the time it has taken to deal with such betrayal I find most troubling.

Finally, I cannot understand the apparent secrecy with which the matter has been handled. Again, please do not get me wrong. I am not wanting the principal destroyed nor made a public spectacle, but I would have thought the clergy of the diocese and staff of the college could at least have been informed that the charges had been laid, what procedures had been adopted, when the outcome was expected. No doubt many who have been concerned or heard rumours have spoken to you directly. What may not be so apparent is that others have come to us or to their parish clergy (rumours about the principal go back a long way). When they have come we have not had the kind of minimum information that would have allowed us to give the straight and sufficient answer we believe we ought to have been able to provide. As you will understand, this has put us in an invidious position, the outcomes have been most unsatisfactory. Also, as the members of our rural deanery have suggested, it has created a situation where even when the matter has been resolved, there can be conjecture and innuendo, and the women who complained remain vulnerable to accusations of exaggerating the issue and acting vindictively. That, of course, should it happen, would be totally unfair.

In this connection, let me say I am not minimising the difficulty of the situation the church has found itself in. I can see how what has appeared as secrecy could have arisen from compassion, the desire not to spoil the principal's chances of making a fresh start. Again, I am not suggesting the matter be put before the general public. I like to think I too could be compassionate. But I have to ask whether offering compassion at this point is either productive or appropriate. As I understand it, the principal has yet to acknowledge to those he has wronged, most seriously the women but also his fellow clergy, how badly he has wronged them. It is true he has been unable to stave off resignation, which must be painful. But that is not the issue. It would seem to me that offering compassion before someone has acknowledged to those they have wronged the fact they have wronged them has precisely the wrong effect. Instead of enabling a fresh start, it lets them get by without seriously admitting the reality of what they've done, allows them, in fact encourages them, to treat their wrong as escapable, and to remain essentially as they were. You may think me hard to say this, but I believe it to be so. In fact I believe it is common sense, Christian, ultimately compassionate: compassion that does not start from justice does not promote renewal, it only confirms what has been.

Not only is compassion without such acknowledgement unproductive, it seems to me inappropriate. There are those, I gather, complaining at the lack of charity in the way the principal has been dealt with, demanding it is time to be forgiving. I too hope there will be a time of forgiveness. But when someone has sinned against the body as a whole, he cannot be forgiven by part of the body only, especially when those who have been wronged most seriously have yet to be asked if they too can forgive. (I am not speaking here of a meeting of equals mutually to resolve an unfortunate blunder. I am speaking of a serious acknowledgement of the wrong, a serious request for forgiveness, and a time for those asked to consider their response.) Again, you may think me hard to see it as I do, but to treat the matter otherwise seems to me to trivialise it.

I hope, Sir, you will not take offence at my writing in this way; though that is a risk I am willing to take. As I say, I do not imagine I know all the issues, I am willing to be corrected where I am wrong. But I have written as I have because the questions that concern me are real and serious; and though I write simply for myself, I know there are others who feel as much as I do.

I would also like to think that the kind of concerns I am expressing, if they have weight, might be picked up and discussed, with a view to formulating guidelines for dealing with similar such emergencies in the future.

Bishop M replied to the Reverend John Shallcrass explaining that he had been very conscious of some of the points that John had raised in his letter and that if he had known all the details that he now knew, he would probably have acted differently. He said that he had been in regular contact with the archbishop because of the provincial implications, particularly in relation to the Prayer Book since R was the chairman of the Prayer Book Commission, and that he had also been advised by the chancellor on important legal matters. He excused himself by saying that these two factors had put some constraint on what they were able to do and on the time that it had taken to deal with a number of issues.

THREE

Meetings with the church hierarchy

Four months had passed since we had submitted our complaints. Nothing had been straightforward or easy. Not that we expected it to be with such a controversial issue as this, but I do not think that any of us had bargained for the ingrained protection of the church towards the male gender and the attitude of the church authorities towards women. It is hard to define this attitude. I could use words such as distrust, suspicion, hatred, loathing, despising or horror, but none of these words exactly pinpoints the *cause* of the antagonism that was directed towards us.

It was also a struggle for the church. It was made hard for them by their desire to protect the church and the desire to protect a fellow clergyman. We did not feel that the church, which had survived for 2000 years, needed protecting. In fact, we thought that the church needed to be reminded to keep its own house in order before it could preach morality and justice to the world. We also strongly believed that, knowing as we did that men will always protect men in spite of the destruction caused to women, the church should no longer be a sanctuary for men only and that we women, as priests of the church, were entitled to protection on the same basis as the male clergy.

The women complainants were invited to a meeting at the bishop's house on 20 December 1989. We agreed that all of us had to be there, since our only resource was our group strength. If only one or two of us were present there was a danger that we could be set up by the bishop; we were only just beginning to understand the strength of the opposition and the nature of the power that we had challenged. As it was, there seemed to be a few anomalies in the arrangements made by the bishop. The people we had been invited to take along to support us were subject to the bishop's approval prior to the meeting, but he chose his own support people without consultation with us. The two people who supported him were, strangely enough, the same people who supported R. We were aware, therefore, that we would not be meeting on equal ground but only on conditions that had the approval of the bishop. Nevertheless, we agreed to his proposal because we needed this opportunity to present our case.

We put together a list of objectives for the meeting. These were

- that the bishop agree to apologise to the women and families who had been affected
- that men and women clergy meet to define their boundaries of behaviour to one another
- that future editions of the Prayer Book not include the name of R as the chairman of the commission
- that R's licence be removed because it is sacramentally offensive that he still remain a priest
- that the disciplinary board take action
- that the women not be blamed
- that the bishop make a statement either to all the clergy of the province or to the diocese in general through Anglican Action
- that if these conditions were not complied with, the women would be free to go to the press.

Before the meeting, two of the women complainants had written to the bishop requesting that he make a public statement indicating that the situation was extremely serious and not a minor matter, that the women who had complained showed courage and were concerned for the good of the whole church, and that procedures would be put in place so that any future incidents of sexual harassment could be dealt with long before they became as complex and serious as this one had become. These three factors were the bottom line for the complainants. It had become quite clear to us that the bishop was not neutral and he was seen to be supporting R by his refusal to act.

We all met together for lunch before the meeting to discuss what we saw as significant outcomes and to pray together for the strength that we needed for this difficult encounter. Two more women who had experienced R's sexually predatory behaviour joined us, although they had not put in formal complaints, and we welcomed them with open arms.

When we arrived at the bishop's house we knocked at the door. I stood there with one of the new members of our group and my approved support person. The bishop opened the door and angrily informed me that he had allocated and approved entry for only one support person and that I may not have another. He stood in the doorway and refused us entry saying that he would not permit this new person to enter his house for the meeting. We explained to him that this new person was not my supporter but that she was a complainant in her own right. He shut the door and went back to his supporters in the room to confer. After some time, he opened the door again and allowed us entry only as far as the bottom of the stairs in the dark hallway. By this time everyone had arrived and we were all made to wait for a long time while the other party discussed the matter in the meeting room. The temptation to leave was strong.

However, our negotiating tool was handed to us: when the door opened briefly, one of our group noted with interest that there was a person in the room who was not on the bishop's list of people permitted to attend the meeting. The bishop had allowed someone who was not on the list to attend the meeting, but he was refusing to allow us to have an extra person inside. That seemed unfair to us, so it was negotiated that either both of them go or they both stay. The bishop was reluctant to exclude his extra person, who was there to support R, and so, after an hour, it was agreed that the new complainants be allowed to attend the meeting. Finally, we were allowed to enter.

The bishop and his party maintained this spirit of antagonism throughout the meeting. The tables were turned on us. We were accused of launching a witch-hunt. We were accused of deliberately organising an orchestrated litany of lies to persecute R who, they claimed, was an angel and a saint who could do no wrong. We were forced into the position of having to defend our complaints. We carefully explained to the self-appointed judge and jury that there was another side to R, one that was problematic for churchwomen, and that it was this sexually predatory behaviour of his that we were reporting, as the dean had suggested, using the legal processes of the church. We said that we believed that we were taking responsibility for other women who could become future victims of R's increasingly flagrant sexuality and that this was a problem the diocese had to deal with.

We realised that we, the women complainants, were the ones on trial here. We were the ones sitting under the judgement of the diocese in this confrontation, not R. We were in a kangaroo court. We were denied a bishops' court and instead experienced a court with judge and jury vehemently opposed to us. To think that we had innocently thought the bishop and his friends would acknowledge the problem and deal with it! We did not anticipate that we would be put on the stand and made to defend ourselves. We had to be clear over and over again that it was not us on trial but R and, if there was going to be a division in the church over this, that R was responsible for it, not us. We had claimed that sexual harassment was not appropriate behaviour in the church. At this meeting it appeared that we were wrong. It would have seemed at that meeting that sexual harassment was, on the contrary, most acceptable behaviour.

Another concern raised was the issue of confidentiality in the counselling situation. We believed that the counsellors who were aware of these situations should not hold the information to themselves but that it was their duty to empower their clients to report the matter to the bishop. We asked for clear guidelines for ethical behaviour. We also requested that processes to deal properly with complaints of this nature be incorporated into the church structure, since it was clear that the church had no idea how to deal with it. The stumbling block caused by the two-year clause in the canons was addressed and it was made clear to the bishop that he had failed in his responsibility to ask all of the complainants whether they had been sexually harassed by R within the last two years. We said that two of us had been harassed within that time limit, which would mean that the bishop could call a bishops' court to enquire into the matter.

The outcome of the meeting was that the bishop would publish a statement to all clergy in the diocese outlining the situation and commending the women for their courage in reporting the matter. In order to ensure that this was done, the women said that if the bishop did not make this statement then the women would be free to make a press statement.

The first copy was a draft document for discussion only and contained the rider 'This is the bishop's proposed statement and is the adaptation of a statement produced by the women after a meeting at the bishop's house on 20 December 1989':

Proposal for a statement on sexual harassment

During the recent media interest in matters of sexual harassment in the church, both Archbishop D and I clearly stated that any complaints of sexual harassment would be taken seriously.

Several specific and serious complaints have been received and followed up. As one consequence of the whole situation a person concerned has left the church's employment.

In line with other institutions and professions, and following recommendations of the Ordained Women's Conference, this and other dioceses and the Provincial Board of Ministry are setting up clear guidelines for dealing with any future complaints of sexual

> harassment. In addition, opportunities will be taken to encourage those in the church to develop understanding and skills in this area.
>
> I wish to commend the courage of those who raised these issues—this was not an attack on an individual. The situation came to my attention as a result of concerns and hurts experienced by a number of people. We should not under-estimate the depth of suffering experienced by all involved in this unhappy situation. Independent counselling has been offered to those most affected.
>
> My prayers continue for healing and for growth, and new understanding in our pilgrimage as the women and men of God.

At that meeting we agreed to meet with Bishop P (a woman) and Archbishop D in the New Year. Minutes of the 20 December meeting were circulated among the women to ensure that everyone was on board with the issues that had arisen at that meeting. There was some dispute about what should be done with these minutes, since they gave the names of the women who had spoken. With some reluctance the women complainants and their support people decided after reading them to destroy the minutes. This is an indication of the fear in which we lived. Everyone was afraid of so many things: the affect on our careers and our private lives, and vendettas and discrimination against us should the minutes get into the wrong hands.

In the *Clergy News* on 5 January 1990 it was announced that R was to leave the college early in February.

✣

The next meeting—with Archbishop D, Bishop P from the Dunedin Diocese, Bishop M and Bishop-elect Dean D—was scheduled for late January 1990. It was not clear whether this group was intended to be a formally established court of bishops, which according to the statutes and canons of the church must be called to hear complaints of this nature about actions that had taken place within the past two years. In other words, we were not clear whether Bishop M's error in asking only two of the complainants whether or not they had been harassed within the last two years was now officially being rectified.

I received a letter from Bishop M telling me that my three support people had been cut down to one. It was obvious that he either failed to understand or refused to believe that one of the new complainants was not my support person but was present in her own right to complain about her treatment by R. I had to explain to him again in writing that she had been present on her own account, having experienced sexual harassment from R, that this had been carefully explained to him at the last meeting, and that there were too many assumptions and presuppositions floating around and these required time and care to talk through and to clear.

He also asked in the letter that we come to the meeting with 'open hearts towards each other'. We laughed at this. How could we possibly come to this meeting with an open heart since the archbishop had made wild accusations against us in the press? How could we possibly meet with 'open hearts' after our last antagonistic meeting where we encountered the bishop's opposition to us? I wrote to the bishop, saying: 'It may be difficult to work constructively with him (the archbishop) when he has judged us so harshly. My fear is that this meeting is a substitute for an ecclesiastical court. I would prefer an ecclesiastical court to this.'

The meeting was heavily weighted in terms of senior members of the church hierarchy. The archbishop, two bishops, the dean, who was the bishop-elect, and two archdeacons were arraigned against six women priests and four laywomen. However, we knew that we had an ally in Bishop P, for she was known for her support of women and the quality of her judgement.

Bishop M opened the meeting with a bible reading and with prayers for hearing each other with open hearts and for reconciliation. The process for the meeting was discussed and agreed upon. We were confused about the difference between resolution and reconciliation. We wanted some *resolution* to this matter in the form of proper processes being put into place for future complaints and also for the diocese to believe the women when they complained. It became evident throughout the meeting that what Bishop M and the archbishop wanted was *reconciliation.* For us reconciliation was sending a confused message. Who were we to be reconciled with in the first place? Were we to be reconciled with ourselves and reconciled to the fact that this is how men normally behave and we should accept this behaviour as a norm? Or reconciled with the bishop? Or with the people who had vehemently opposed us in favour of a man who was sexually abusive? Or were we expected to be reconciled with the man who had sexually abused us? We were very puzzled. It appeared that the authorities wanted to smooth the whole business over and carry on as though it had never happened, even though they did not know what had happened. Their focus of attention had been concentrated on the *validity* of our complaints according to the canons and the statutes of the church, and they had done their best to declare that our complaints were invalid because of the two-year clause.

Someone expressed bewilderment at what was meant by 'sexual harassment'. What sort of behaviour were we complaining about? This was the first time in the six months that had passed that anyone had dared to ask us what had actually happened. In the meantime we women had been verbally abused and persecuted by other church members and made victims of the church's insane desire to protect the status quo at the expense of the mental, spiritual, emotional and physical injury to many of its members.

We women glanced at each other in surprise. I knew the dean had written a report when I had told him my story, because I had read it. It was now apparent that he had not told anyone else of its contents. He knew what had happened and because he had not passed on this written first-hand evidence of what he himself had called 'atrocities', he had allowed us to be persecuted. He had kept the evidence to himself. He had kept the church hierarchy, those who claimed to judge us, in ignorance of the facts.

Suddenly I realised that we had to tell our stories again. It was a difficult decision to make at that point. How much information about our personal experiences could we reveal to this august assembled body? One complainant had firmly stated that, rather than tell her full story, she would reveal publicly only what was the minimum requirement of the Human Rights Commission. She did this, and I respected her right to do so. Another told a different story to the one she had revealed to me when I first asked her. These two women's evidence did not constitute the degree of sexual abuse that I had experienced and it dawned on me that if I did not fully explain the behaviour I had experienced, there was a distinct possibility that the matter would not be taken seriously. I was concerned for the truth to be known, so I told about R's sexual advances.

Shock waves went around the room when I asked whether it was appropriate behaviour for a male priest to expose himself in a church or in a public place. Two of the other women also stated that R had exposed himself to them in churches and public places. At last the bishops understood that there was indeed a problem. Someone asked one of the complainants what she had done when he had exposed himself to her in a church. She replied that she was very embarrassed and did not know what to do. The archbishop attempted to justify this behaviour by asking what was abnormal about it. I asked him whether he himself engaged in similar behaviour. He denied that he did, but continued to ask if this was indeed abnormal behaviour. The complainant again explained to us how she felt about staying in conference centres while working together on church projects, when R would arrange to have his bedroom next to hers. She said that she had requested protection from other committee members without revealing the nature of the problems that she was experiencing with him.

The archbishop stated that the church had its own law, which was separate and different from secular law. He said that as priests of the church we did not have recourse to civil law and that judgement would be meted out by the law of the church. He then informed us that the law of the church differed from civil law in that it was concerned with forgiveness and reconciliation rather than with prosecution and punishment. He commanded us to work within the law of the church.

We were left with no redress. Civil law had been denied us and we were to submit to the law of the church. We had become victims of the church twice over. First we had been sexually abused by a priest of the church. Now we were held tightly in the claws of the church and asked to forgive the unforgivable. The church had proved itself incapable of following its own law as it is written in its own statutes and canons. On false grounds, the church had denied us access to a bishops' court to judge the matter. The church itself had handed us over to the judgement of the college board of governors, which is a nominally secular body. They in turn had failed to follow the correct protocols of civil law and had allowed R to resign his position, and had generously compensated him for his resignation. We were not yet ready to fulfil the law of forgiveness and reconciliation. We felt that it was too soon and that there was a process in the act of forgiveness that required the activity of both parties. To this end we requested the bishop to ask R to write letters of apology to us and to our families for the chaos and destruction that he had caused in our lives. Without his acknowledgement of the pain and suffering that he had caused we were unable to forgive him. We women said that if he did not apologise to us we would go to the press again. We, in turn, were compelled into an agreement that we would not go to the press without prior consultation with the bishop, who would approve what had been written by us before it was published.

After the meeting, we women stayed and talked. Bishop P congratulated us on our stand, commenting on the strength of the Christchurch women. I had not met her before and found her clarity and incisiveness of judgement impressive. She promised that she would ensure that all the bishops would be made aware of the issues. We all agreed that it was a horrible meeting and it had taken a huge amount of our energy. We also realised that this meeting had been the equivalent of an ecclesiastical court and that, because R had resigned his position at the college and had left the city, a true ecclesiastical court could not now be called.

✣

It was suggested that the Chapel of the Upper Room at the college be cleansed with water and with prayer to rid it of the bad memories and to claim the chapel back for goodness and for God. We were all enthusiastic about this. It had been difficult to enter the college without feeling nauseous. To go there together in a group with the specific intention of cleansing would break that barrier, that feeling of deep reluctance we all experienced when we returned.

I was not able to be present when the women gathered together in the Chapel of the Upper Room for the cleansing ritual. They told me that they had filled a large and beautiful blue and white china bowl with water and sprinkled it over the floor to purge the space of contamination. They had prayed together and gained new strength. A few days later, I ventured back to the college on my own to participate in the cleansing ceremony and to sprinkle some water around for myself. But there was no water left in the bowl. I wondered what I could do to make clean this dramatic space.

I wandered around this white, stark, monastic chapel and looked at the paintings on the wall, a series of original works that together form the stations of the cross. There is such pain on the face of the crucified Christ, the twisted thorns on his head, the blood and sweat on his hair as he hangs forever on the cross that we created for him. I understood at last the agony of the body of Christ; it is the church that still condemns this Christ of ours to eternal pain.

We continue to crucify Christ. We continue to inflict pain on that body by perpetuating injustice and by persecuting those who seek justice. This body of Christ, this church, had, like the garment of Jesus, been rent asunder. We all hung in agony on the cross along with Christ.

R was a tortured man with the pain of his own sick perversions. He had caused us all so much pain, just this one man. He had destroyed lives, marriages and careers. He had raped and sexually assaulted women. He had carelessly broken down moral codes. For these offences against the women of the church, he had refused to accept responsibility. He had caused his own crucifixion, the crucifixion of other members of that body and of the body itself.

We women, too, hung upon that cross, tortured and persecuted first by the agony of a man who was out of control and second by the very institution that claims to offer righteousness and salvation. We were the latest manifestations of the women who have been persecuted, exploited, rendered inferior and subordinated by men of the church throughout the ages. This is how men had always treated educated, strong women who threatened their power by refusing to stay silent and by insisting on justice. We are fortunate to live in an age when burning at the stake is out of favour. We had jolted the power balance of the church by breaking the silence and speaking out about behaviour that destroyed women. We took the risk of sacrificing ourselves on behalf of future generations of women, to free them from exploitative behaviour that could prevent them from reaching their full potential in the church, and, who knows, perhaps they would at last be able to claim their full humanity in the church.

ii. of power and spirituality
iii. of clergy roles as perceived by clergy and client.

c. providing the opportunity of discreet help for those who sense themselves to be at risk in this matter.
d. making recommendation for professional supervision for clergy to promote growth in self-awareness and pastoral skills.

The committee acknowledges all the contributions which have been submitted via the bishop, and in particular the work of Chris Cherry and Carolyn Brewer, and that of the previous *ad hoc* committee which began the work.

We submit the accompanying material for discussion and comment. It is at this stage very much a draft document.

What is Sexual Harassment?

Sexual harassment describes the situation where a person is the unwilling recipient of persistent deliberate sexual overtures or innuendo by means of any of the senses. (The committee understands one incident to be inappropriate behaviour; more than one incident to be harassment.) It can include:

- Offensive joking, comments, teasing, or abuse about sexual matters.
- Offensive cartoons, cards, presents, etc, of a sexual nature.
- Rude gestures, comments, or leering.
- Display of pornographic pictures or material.
- Unwanted, deliberate physical contact, such as patting, pinching, brushing up against you, or kissing.
- Repeated requests for dates.
- Requests or demands for sex (which may include threats, or promises about future achievement/employment, etc).
- Following you home, or constant phone calls at home or office.
- Direct sexual violence such as rape or assault.

Sexual harassment has more to do with the way power is used in our society, whether personal or structural power, than with social or romantic relations which may develop between two people. 'No individual is likely to be harassed by unwelcome sexual behaviour if they can quite freely reject that behaviour'. (Riggs, Sharn. 'Sexual Power in the Workplace', *New Zealand Times,* 6 April 1986)

Sexual harassment is a powerful way for men to undermine and control women. There is an implicit (and sometimes explicit) message that the refusal to comply with the harasser's demands will lead to employment or study related reprisals.

Sexual harassment can drive women out of a particular vocation, or out of a particular course of study, by creating a hostile, intimidating or pressured environment.

'Like women who are raped, sexually harassed women feel humiliated, degraded, ashamed, embarrassed and cheap, as well as angry'. (MacKinnon, Catherine A. *Sexual Harassment of Working Women: A Case of Sex Discrimination*, Yale University Press, Newhaven and London, 1979, p.47)

While it is acknowledged that sexual harassment can come from a person of either sex against a person of the opposite or same sex, the most common situation involves a male superior and a female subordinate. As Aggarwal commented: 'Sexual harassment…is…a comprehensive pattern of hostile behaviour meant to underscore women's difference from and, by implication, inferiority with respect to the dominant male group.' (Aggarwal, Arjun P. *Sexual Harassment in the Workplace*, Butterworths, Toronto and Vancouver, 1987, p.5)

What To Do if you Believe you are Being Sexually Harassed:

1. Remember, sexual harassment is illegal. You are not to blame. No matter how complicated the situation is, the harasser is responsible for the abuse.
2. If you think you are being sexually harassed, talk to someone you trust. It is important to talk it over and get support. This

support might come from someone in your family, a friend, or someone with whom you work. Remember, you are not alone.

3. Let the harasser know as clearly, directly and explicitly as possible that you are not interested in his/her attentions. If you do this in writing keep a copy of your letter/s. You may use your trusted friend as a witness.
4. Document what happens. Keep a diary; save any notes or pictures from the harasser—don't throw them away in anger. Write down specific times, dates, places, kinds of incidents, your responses, his/her answers, any witnesses.
5. If the harasser refuses to acknowledge the problem and modify his/her behaviour and you feel you need to take the matter further, use the diocesan procedures. The diocesan procedures are designed to produce an immediate and thorough investigation.
6. If you are not satisfied with the result of the diocesan investigation, you may take the matter further by using the Human Rights Commission.

Diocesan Procedures for Dealing with Allegations of Sexual Harassment

The complainant should approach a senior diocesan person of their choice. The diocese will appoint a panel of clergy (or possibly lay people).

1. The appointed diocesan representative will appoint two people, one male and one female, to interview the person making the complaint. They will then hear the response of the person accused. This series of interviews should happen as soon as possible.
2. The two interviewers will consult with the senior diocesan representative on the outcome of their interviews. Except for clearly unavoidable reasons, this process from the first report to this consultation must not be more than seven days.
3. The senior diocesan representative will move to call the two parties together, each with a supporting friend, and the meeting

conducted by a mediator appointed. Again, every effort will be made to see that this meeting occurs within seven days.

4. The advocate will then advise the bishop and a resolution will be sought which is acceptable to all concerned. This may include ongoing supervision and/or counselling.
5. If a satisfactory conclusion is not reached, it is possible for either party to proceed through the facilities of the Human Rights Commission.

In June 1991 the Provincial Board for Ministry (Tikanga Pakeha) put out a document entitled *Sexual Harassment: An Issue for the Church*. It took the church nearly two years to accept that there was an issue and to deal with it seriously. It took enormous effort from many people to come up with appropriate processes to manage the tidal wave that swept over it.

The women who gave voice to what might have hitherto been considered to be a matter of intense privacy must be hailed as heroines of the New Age of the church. They have served not only the women of the past who have been sexually abused and exploited by predatory males, those who used the church as a cover for their insatiable desires, but they have also served the women of the future who will be believed and protected from this sort of perversion, which has existed in the church for too long. The senior members of the Diocese of Christchurch, who were thrust into an extraordinary crisis, struggled to understand the nature of sexual harassment at the same time as they struggled to protect their friend and their church.

In 1996 the Christchurch Diocese announced the appointment of an Anglican Diocesan Monitor who was contracted to work under the ethical guidelines established in 1995. The guidelines were to cover all clergy, lay workers and members of the church who hold positions of responsibility and who act on behalf of the church. By 1996 there had been nine complaints of 'inappropriate behaviour'.

FOUR

The struggle to understand

The church hierarchy and the secular world struggled to come to terms with what sexual harassment really meant. It chose to use this term rather than that of sexual abuse, or the abuse of power, which is what it really was. It took time for both the church and the secular world to stop running away from the problem, minimising it, hiding its head in the sand, pretending that it was normal and justifiable behaviour for men to indulge their fantasies on women and that to be a 'red-blooded' male was a social norm.

The question of power was beginning to be addressed as the major component of sexual harassment. Once again the Reverend John Shallcrass tackled this hard nut from his perspective as a male employee of the college, teaching theology. He struggled to understand the issue of power and how it was exercised by R, whom he had known since they were students together. In a private letter to a colleague at the time, John speculated at length how R achieved the power he had over others, and why none of them had realised what he'd been getting up to. John Shallcrass, too, as an employee of the college, had been subject to R's abuse of power; but as Shallcrass was a man rather than a woman that abuse was devoid of sexual content and as such left him free to search for an understanding about the way R used his power.

In reference to R's use of power, John commented on the way in which he felt manipulated in staff meetings. There were two background factors that allowed R to wield power over him. The first was that R presented himself as having absolute authority over John, and constantly reminded John that he was a paid servant of the college and thus was ultimately answerable to the college. Yet, when it came down to a base level, R, too, was a paid servant of the college. The other factor that was at play in this game of power was John's self-confessed need to hold his job and succeed in making it work.

Evidently R would use threatening silences—silences with an interested, puzzled, pleading look on his face, but silences that were nevertheless extremely threatening. John could not understand why R used silence as a power tool; he could not understand how much of this stemmed from the fact that R had nothing to contribute, or to what extent it was a deliberate ploy to keep John on the wrong foot. But R would sit there, as a combination of employer, colleague, friend and therapist, and expect John to come up with the goods. The first thing R did in their meetings was get out his clipboard, flip a new page and sit with his pen poised! Because of John's need to prove that he was succeeding, even though he knew how phoney it all was, he would make an offering to start the conversation. But R would sit silent. John would then feel that he had not measured up. John would then make a further offering to the conversation even though he felt that he was talking too much, complicating the issue and compromising himself. R would sit silent. And so the game continued.

John said he did not think that this was simply stupidity on his own part. He wrote, 'It seems to me the essence of conversation is one person's reaching out to find the partner, in the trust that the partner will be there reaching out to them. When the partner consistently refuses to be known, sits withdrawn, hiding, the natural reaction is panic: What's going on? Why am I failing where usually I succeed? What am I doing wrong? I think it was this panic that led me to keep talking and talking, exposing myself to supercilious scorn, getting myself in a mess, and knowing I was doing it; blaming myself at the time, and only subsequently registering that I'd been manipulated again.' Eventually, John decided to try out another way of communicating with R by reflecting his behaviour back to him and offering nothing to the conversation on the grounds that if R would not come to meet him then John would not try to meet R. John experimented on him, allowing R to float an 'intellectual' conversation to which John would begin to contribute, then he would stop and leave the next move to R, 'which left him tie-tugging, pipe-sucking, paper-rearranging, window-gazing, and Sherlock Holmes carpet-walking…'

As to why no-one had ever picked up on his more nefarious activities, John's simple explanation was that he did not think that anyone would ever take R seriously because he thought that practically everyone could see that he was so patently a fraud that they imagined he was harmless. He wrote: 'We were a bunch of Hindenburgs sneering at the little Austrian painter, thinking him a fool, fondly imagining fools do no harm.' John, in a more serious vein, understood that he had eventually reached the age where he realised that fooling about as R fooled about, fantasising, flirting, refusing to be serious, was stupid and destructive. Because John himself had passed through this life phase, even though he admitted that it was often a struggle, it had never occurred to him that R was doing anything more than still foolishly flirting. John noted that R's ability to act the fool was the perfect cover. Everybody knew that R had all these relationships, but they all took it for granted there was nothing much in them, knowing what they all knew about grown-up life. After all, John said, 'it's only the House Fool—only R just being R, pipe and suit and no longer pipe and duffle-coat, but the same pretentious Primo Don, needing even now to prove to the world he is as much to be reckoned with as anyone else. How wrong we were. We thought he'd grown up, and he hadn't. The 'Rev R Pan'. Sneering at us behind our backs. Which I imagined we sensed but didn't care about. Till we realised things were serious.'

John stepped from a psychological analytical framework into a theological analysis of R. He considered R to be the purest example he knew of Kierkegaard's Aesthetic—the one still in childhood who lives from the givenness of the moment, responding to what happens and, in a more advanced form of the syndrome, also manipulating what happens for the gratification the moment gives. 'He is extremely quick and subtle, but he is an extremely subtle and quick child who cries because of what has happened to him, not at what he has done. They are the tears of a child who has been denied the cookie jar.' John believed that R had yet to fall out of the Aesthetic into the Ethical, yet to become aware of himself as related to the principles of Right and Wrong, as related to himself as embracing his past and his future, as related to others as embodying blessing and obligation. John wrote: 'Until he falls into the Ethical, until he acknowledges that he has not been denied the cookie jar, been both serious obligation and serious blessing, any offer of compassion, counselling or whatever, seems to me worse than useless.' John's theological framework for analysis moderated his anger towards R, though not his anger at what R had done to others or the way the church had been reluctant to deal with it. His commentary was the beginning of the hard task of reflection and analysis in an attempt to understand how a man such as R could achieve high status in an institution such as the church.

✣

In the meantime, the June 1990 edition of *Anglican Action*, the newsletter for the Christchurch Diocese, announced in major headlines that the guidelines to deal with sexual harassment as had been requested by the Ordained Women's Conference were nearly completed and that each diocese was being encouraged to set up its own machinery. Ten months later the fact that serious sexual abuse had occurred within the diocese and that five written complaints had been made was still being kept secret from the lay people in the church. The article continued the lie by saying that a number of claims of sexual harassment had been made in the North Island but only one complaint had been made in the Christchurch Diocese and that the parties had been counselled. This was minimisation and a soothing hand, as of a parent to a child, to hide the real extent of the problem by telling church people, the very people who needed protection, that everything was under control and that the problem lay elsewhere—not in our patch, not in our backyard. The article attempted some analysis of the problem, reporting that it was not a case of seduction but of the misuse of power. A woman priest was reported as saying that the problem occurs when a woman feels powerless to deal with authority being wielded by a male superior, and justified it by saying that it was more probably due to insensitivity than deliberate sexual harassment. Ken McMaster, who used to run the anger management courses for Anglican Social Services, supported this woman priest's summary of why this happened, saying that men were just having a bit of fun and did not see their behaviour as a problem because they did not set out to harass women and did not perceive that women would find their behaviour offensive. He said that men were excused because many of them did not know how to communicate in appropriate ways and consider that what they do is normal and flattering. McMaster said that if men do set out to harass it is because they feel threatened by women and that it was possible for men to change by learning to base relationships on respect and equality. This was a shocking attitude for a professional counsellor to take. McMaster placed the problem of sexual harassment firmly on the shoulders of the women, accusing women of not being able to cope with authority, accusing mothers of not teaching their sons how to treat women, and blaming women for their threatening behaviour towards men. It was disgraceful and not at all related to the situation that we had confronted.

In July 1990, another of R's victims emerged, a woman who

had been sexually abused when she was being counselled by him at the age of seventeen. The Reverend Patricia Allan wrote to the archbishop to tell him about this new revelation and at the same time asked him why the church had sanctioned R's appointment as provost of the college for Asian students in Palmerston North, which gave him continuing access to vulnerable young women. She exclaimed: 'To believe his promise of reformation without any real trial period seems incredible.' Patricia bravely confronted the issue of the archbishop's intention to re-licence R after six months.

> Please sir, will you listen to the cries of the women who were wronged by him...like this one from Dunedin; like the ones you met in Christchurch; like the two whose stories I heard with horror in Waiapu in March. Know that because of his golden handshake from the college and his current lucrative position in Palmerston North there is already for many men and women a deep sense of injustice and betrayal. To re-licence him as a functioning priest of the church will exacerbate this sense to possibly unmanageable heights. I have absolutely no intention or wish to threaten or blackmail you, but one clergy journalist told me it would be the story of the decade. The possibility of disclosure to the media is still real. My prayers are for you and all the other bishops as you continue to work through the implications of R's years of unrestrained misuse of power.

She sent copies of this letter to all of the Bishops in New Zealand to ensure that the archbishop did not lose it in his filing system.

The archbishop requested a meeting of the women together with R in Wellington for the purpose of reconciliation. Four women flew up to Wellington for the day to meet with the archbishop, R and his psychotherapist. I did not go; I felt that I was still too emotionally battered and did not feel ready to be reconciled with him, for my anger was still huge. Nor did I believe that reconciliation could occur with R before he had apologised, offering some indication that he understood the seriousness of his predatory sexual behaviour. Even if he had apologised and expressed his repentance it would have taken me some time to forgive him, if I ever could. Reconciliation in my mind could only take place after the difficult process of repentance and forgiveness. To seek for reconciliation at this stage was too early for me, and I reckoned that I would not be in a position to further the conversation in any constructive way.

I only have second-hand reports of that meeting. Any honest discussion was thwarted by the presence of R's psychotherapist, so no progress or headway was made. The archbishop had put himself in the position of mediator without consent by the women. It was a very inappropriate position for him to take since he had publicly insulted the women through the avenue of the media and, added to this, he was a close friend of R. Once again, in a situation where every care ought to have been taken to ensure total equality in the balance of power, the balance, either through thoughtlessness or deliberately, was tipped in favour of both the hierarchy and the offender. One would have been forgiven for thinking that an archbishop might have been aware of this and taken precautions to ensure that the meeting was balanced enough to succeed in its intention. As it was, there was no way that progress could have been made. After a frustrating day, the women had to return home without achieving reconciliation.

The issue of power became a generalised topic to be examined in and of itself as it applied to the church structures. In an idle moment one woman priest drew a cynical, composite picture of how she believed the diocese distributed power amongst its members. To begin with, she said, there are

> those who have power and are trying to hold onto it, either by being very controlling (including controlling how change happens, instead of listening to those who are without power) or very ineffective (blocking anything through incompetence) or starting to

> panic and calling for moderation whenever those who haven't had power begin to get it for a while. There are those who say commendable things (for example, that the church must change in order to share ministry with women) but do nothing, especially when faced with temptation—such as a mitre. There are those who function like satellites circulating round the big planets, massaging the egos of those with power and benefiting from the support and patronage. These include those who are beginning to climb the career ladder—for example, the young male clergy who feel very threatened by women clergy, whose approach and experience is different; those older women who chose to behave a certain way a decade ago in order to get ordained and are enjoying the benefits too much to make changes; and those younger women who support the men near them to give themselves protection in a system where the visible power is held by those who are white, male and ordained. The final layer is comprised of those who don't fit, who don't benefit much from the present situation and who understand their own experience of marginalisation.

She concluded that the power bloc could only be broken by those on the outside fringes uniting in order to work consultatively, collectively and analytically and with a very clear focus. The combined experience of the strength, wisdom and theology of those on the edge of the institution who have an awareness of the situation can strategise for change. Change, she said, does not just happen; it comes from strategies and those with power are certainly strategising to keep it.

✣

At synod held in February 1990, the Reverend Ken Davy, who was the co-ordinator of Marriage Guidance in South Canterbury and assistant priest in the parish of Kensington-Otipua, called for ethical guidelines to be drawn up because he was alarmed about improper sexual relationships between counselling clergy and their clients. He asked that a ministry commission in consultation with the bishop draw up the guidelines. Ken Davy expressed his concerns about the quality of ministry and counselling that some people were receiving, because some counsellors had ambivalent attitudes towards sexual relationships with people seeking guidance. People seeking counselling were vulnerable, and any improper relationships that could result were a distortion of power. He claimed that it was this distortion of power that caused people to feel fearful about facing the issue. He saw that feminism had resulted in women having greater confidence to speak out about the issue, but he did not think it was more prevalent now than in the past.

The *Dominion Sunday Times* of 11 November 1990 made front page headlines of Ken Davy's comments. Eirwen Harris interviewed him and reported him as saying that some male Anglican priests were having sex with women who had sought their help on marriage and personal problems, and these priests had used the power they had over their women parishioners to coerce them into sexual relationships. He explained that few women told anyone about these relationships, and they carried the feeling of entrapment for years. Ken Davy said he did not blame the clergymen, who often felt lonely and who were under considerable pressure to help others while repressing their own problems. Often their family life was not supportive because of the pressures of work. These problems arose from the priests' childhood conditioning, their personal problems and the structure of the Anglican Church. These pressures lay dormant until a counsellor became strongly attracted to one of his parishioners, forgot the woman's needs, and used her to heal his own emotional wounds.

> 'Suddenly you are in a situation (with a woman parishioner) where something happens which very strongly turns you on...then you're out of control and into the forbidden zone ...

> 'From the guy's perspective, he completely loses his professional ethics and his responsibilities to the church. And he is focused into the here and now of this woman, whom he sees as something of a goddess, somebody who is going to transform him and heal his wounds. The promise it offers the victim is that she is transformed into somebody who is highly desirable and worthy.'
>
> Mr Davy said that after the first sexual experience the woman begins to realise that the relationship is not meeting her needs. She continues it only because it raises her self-esteem and rarely tells anybody about it, probably because she felt trapped.
>
> When a priest was found out he usually either undertook personal reflection before returning to his work, or followed what Mr Davy said was the Anglican tradition where the incident was not acknowledged and he was transferred to another parish.
>
> He said that evidence that sex offenders would reoffend suggested that once a priest had a relationship with a client he would always have a weakness in that area.
>
> Church selection procedures were strict, but priests received inadequate training on counselling others. The church had to look at clergy selection and to improve training and supervision as well as the establishment of ethical guidelines, he said.

The result of this interview with Ken Davy was that he was chastised by the church hierarchy, who refused to allow him any further access to the media. It was a damage control measure by the church to suppress the voices of its members so that the outside world of lay people were not permitted to know the inner world of the church. It imposed silence not only on the women, but also on the men who saw the predatory sexual behaviour happening and broke the silence in an effort to understand the behaviour and also to warn potential victims what may happen to them if they were engaged in counselling relationships. It was over a year since the Ordained Women's Conference had raised the issue, yet the church was still attempting to silence anyone who wanted to speak out.

On 1 May 1991, *The Press* published a piece from the British *Daily Telegraph* about sexual harassment in the American Protestant Church; the United Methodist Church's General Council on Ministries reported that a recent study had found that 77 per cent of its clergywomen had reported incidents of sexual harassment, and 41 per cent of the cases were ascribed to church colleagues or other clergy. One clergyman wrote: 'The kinds of sexual harassment that disturb me are the actions of my brother clergy, who seem to offer unsolicited looks, touches and comments to the more attractive clergywomen fairly frequently.' The study found that ordained churchwomen seem to be special targets for the harassers, because 23 per cent of lay women had reported incidents of sexual harassment which was less than a third of the percentage of clergywomen.

A smaller survey, conducted by the United Church of Christ in Cleveland among 138 women clergy found that 45 per cent of them said they had been sexually harassed on church precincts, which was considered to be an inordinately high number. The report concluded that it was particularly disturbing that it happened in the church. The Methodist Church study cited nine categories of harassment, ranging from leers and pressure for dates to sexual assault and rape. 'Unsolicited jokes with sexual content' were the most frequently cited form of harassment. Another article in *The Press* reported that the Australian churches had admitted that clergy engaged in sex abuse. Reuters in Sydney reported that church leaders had agreed that some clergymen sexually harassed women, but they rejected claims in an Australian Broadcasting Corporation documentary that about 3000 Australian clergymen were guilty of such behaviour. A television documentary called 'Ultimate Betrayal' said that about 15 per cent, or 3000 of Australia's 20,000 clergymen were involved in sexual harassment.

The Reverend Peter Horsfield, Dean of Melbourne's Uniting Church Theological College, said on the programme that he had spoken to women who describe the effects of pastoral abuse as 'like having been savaged by God' or 'like having your soul stolen'. Melbourne's Centre Against Sexual Assault told the programme it received three telephone calls a week from women claiming sexual abuse by clergymen. A spokeswoman for the centre said that more than 100 women had telephoned since the documentary went on the air to report sexual abuse by clergymen. A Catholic nun, Anne Hall, said the reports ranged from unwanted touching to rape. 'It also often produces spiritual crises, a shattering of their beliefs,' she said. Catholic and Anglican church leaders said they had no evidence of large-scale sexual abuse by clergymen, but the Most Reverend John Bayton, Anglican Archbishop of Geelong, near Melbourne, qualified that by saying that they accepted the fact 'that it has happened, that it is happening and that it will continue to happen'. He disputed the percentage rate that had been given, claiming that it was not an accurate figure since their experience of dealing with sexual assaults indicated that the figure is very much lower. The Anglican Archbishop of Brisbane, the Most Reverend Peter Hollingworth, said clergymen who committed sexual offences against parishioners had psychosexual problems and should be dealt with by the church. 'There is no doubt instances of abuse do occur, as anyone in church leadership will be painfully aware,' he said. Unlike sexual abuse by doctors, lawyers, and psychiatrists, which were dealt with in court, incidents within the church should be handled by clergy disciplinary tribunals. This is not a conspiracy of silence but an attempt to govern our own household.'

In the documentary, Ms Jan Tully, a worker at Melbourne's Centre against Sexual Assault, said women abused by clergy were pressured to remain silent to protect the church. 'We've heard of women going down to the church on a Saturday night to set up flowers and being raped by clergy,' she said. 'Others have accepted lifts home after choir practice from ministers and have been assaulted in the car. The church is not a safe place for women.'

In spite of these revelations on an international scale, the diocese maintained a code of silence. The media continued to be the only avenue through which to expose this widespread problem, a problem that affected not just churchwomen but all women in the workplace. On 2 May 1992, *The Press* reported an interesting altercation between two women members of Parliament. Headed 'Shipley issues harassment warning', it said that the then Minister of Social Welfare, Jenny Shipley, had issued a strong warning to people who found sexual harassment acceptable, saying that sexual harassment is a problem that must be dealt with firmly by both men and women in this country. She stated that it may be fashionable to say that sexual harassment is not a problem for women and that it is a consequence of being participants in the adult world of employment, but she found that attitude unacceptable since women's skills in contributing to the productivity and success of any company or organisation should not be hampered, impeded or undermined by unacceptable sexist behaviour. Mrs Shipley was referring to a speech made by Marie Hasler in which Hasler had declared that women should accept sexual harassment as the price of equality, urging women to withstand pettiness and stating that the monetary compensation awarded by courts for harassment would not help establish the right to equality. Marie Hasler said: 'Women cannot have it both ways; equality where convenient but special consideration when the going gets rough. Equality has its price. That price might be unwelcome sexual advances, irritating jokes and obnoxious colleagues.' These controversial comments drew fire from women's groups and other women MPs. Mrs Shipley said that while women continued to cope individually with sexist behaviour, 'it is entirely inappropriate for sexual harassment to be condoned or written off as trivial'. Mrs Shipley spoke for the government when she said that the Employment Contracts Act ensured women's rights were protected from such behaviour, with procedures for complaints firmly laid down. 'The strong message to women in the work force and employers is that sexual harassment is a serious issue and legislation ensures that workers who are tempted to think that sexual harassment is some sort of recreational pursuit risk being seriously dealt with.'

✣

The women complainants about R's sexually predatory behaviour had suffered under the code of silence imposed by the church. We had not received an apology from R, who was unrepentant and continued to hold us responsible for his downfall. We had a meeting at Patricia Allan's place to see what the next step was going to be. We all decided that R was not the issue any more. We could no longer wait for an apology from him that was never going to come. Even if he did apologise, what sort of apology would it be anyway? It would be dragged out of him, and we would not have the satisfaction of a genuine repentance. In other words, even if he did apologise, could we really believe that it was a genuine act of contrition. At this stage an apology from him now would only be a political act of expediency on his part to gratify the church and to win back his licenses, which the hierarchy were wanting to restore to him.

We unanimously reached the decision that the issue had passed beyond R and that, although he may have been the catalyst for the crisis, he was not the issue any more. The issue had outgrown its origins in the sexually abusive behaviour of R. It had grown into the firm belief that we had a church to bring to accountability, so that it would take responsibility for its members and its own domestic health. R had faded into the background. He became the agent for bringing the problem to the surface. His role was over. Whatever he had done and whatever pain he had caused individuals was now a chapter that was complete. This was a new chapter now, a new level in dealing with this monstrous problem. It was no longer the women versus R, or in fact the women versus any individual. The time had come to reflect on the ideology, the philosophy, the theology of the events that had occurred and to try to make sense out of them for the future. We needed to deal directly with the church and to enable the church members to reflect on the injustice that existed in the only institution in society that pledged to fight injustice, to reflect on its own immorality when its purpose was to preach morality and to reflect on its own patriarchal behaviour at a time when discrimination of any kind is illegal. If it was to be true to its own word, it was time for the church to examine its own structures and change that which needed to be changed. This was a significant shift in the history of this process.

In 1992, the church may have thought that the issue was settled and that everyone could get back to normal. But this was not to be. There were eruptions outside the church community because of the secrecy and the imposed silence. At a health day for the women of Sumner, there was gossip about our situation in the church. Amongst the women present was Amanda Cropp, at that time the only South Island journalist for the *Dominion Sunday Times*. She became curious about the matter and felt strongly that there was a news item there that would be of national interest. The women's network was alive and well, so it did not take her long to track down Patricia Allan as the one who had led us through the process.

Amanda Cropp wanted to talk with all the women who had submitted written complaints to the church and to the college. We women talked the matter through, taking into account the church's imposition of silence upon us and the subsequent negotiated agreement that we would honour this request on the condition that R sent a written apology to each of us. As this had not occurred, we felt free to talk to her. She interviewed each of us separately. We were not sure whether we would be sued for libel but felt that if the matter was going to be taken to court then we would at least be free to clear our names publicly. She, too, realised that there was the possibility of a problem with the law and she undertook to take legal advice to ensure the anonymity of all those concerned. Accordingly we were all given pseudonyms so that we could honestly and truthfully tell the story that the church had never allowed to be heard.

It took a long time for Amanda's article to be published, and we waited as though the sword of Damocles was about to fall on us. The article was finally printed on 17 May 1992. Amanda won a national award for the best piece of investigative journalism for the year and the piece was displayed for a long time in an up-market shopping centre for all to read. The article was headed 'Clergy who enter the Forbidden Zone':

> As a depressed and homesick student living away from home for the first time, nineteen-year-old 'Ann' went to a clergyman for counselling. The weekly chats began innocently enough, but gradually the minister persuaded her to perform sexual acts on him under the guise of teaching her about male sexuality.
>
> Ann never felt comfortable about those secret sessions in his office, but it was a long time before she recognised them as sexual abuse. She knew the married clergyman had a similar relationship with another student yet it was more than twenty years before she realised that they were far from being his only victims.
>
> The clergyman, meanwhile, had gone on to become a respected member of the Anglican Church. Other sources suggest he had relationships with as many as 20 women over the years and even when his misconduct was reported, supporters found it difficult to believe that such a charismatic and gifted priest could have offended in this way. Some took the view that he was the victim of a sustained campaign by a group of vindictive women.
>
> The issue of the clergyman's alleged sexual misconduct was brought to a head by a conference of ordained women. Delegates were told about a young priest who had suffered so much physical harassment during her training that she considered abandoning a career in the church. Soon after this conference this priest, together

with half a dozen other ordained and lay women, laid formal complaints of sexual harassment with the church.

Their actions caused a furore and prompted the Anglican Church to introduce formal procedures for dealing with allegations of sexual harassment. Methodist and Presbyterian churches have adopted similar policies over the past year and the Catholic Church is also considering the matter.

The Anglican document on sexual harassment points out that a woman harassed by a minister often feels intimidated into allowing the unwanted behaviour to continue, especially if he is able to threaten her job security or her reputation.

It also quotes from *Sex in the Forbidden Zone*, a book by American psychiatrist Peter Rutter. According to Rutter, intense feelings about a therapist are part of a psychological phenomenon known as transference and it can last for years after the therapy ends.

He says these intense feelings can occur in other professional settings such as between a divorce lawyer and a distraught woman client, a university lecturer and an honours student, a clergyman and a parishioner.

The key element is the imbalance of power between the two parties. Rutter says sex between male professionals and their female clients is always wrong, no matter who initiates it, or how willing the participants say they are. He argues that because the man has the greater power, he is responsible for preventing unethical sexual contact, regardless of how provocative the woman is.

'In the "forbidden zone" the factors of power, trust and dependency remove the possibility of a woman freely giving consent to sexual contact. Put another way, the dynamics of the forbidden zone can render a woman unable to withhold consent.'

In a bid to deal with clergy straying into the 'forbidden zone' the Anglican church has set up a network of contact people who encourage victims to take action about harassment. They may ask a bishop to intervene, and if the complaint cannot be resolved informally, an outside mediator may be hired to find a satisfactory solution. If this fails the complaint is heard by a grievance committee. Church employees or licenced priests who are accused of sexual harassment can be sacked or their licences terminated if they refuse to take part in mediation or grievance proceedings.

Although they welcome the new guidelines, some of the women who laid complaints against the clergyman are still angry about the way the church reacted to their plight. All requested anonymity because they feared a backlash if publicly identified.

'Helen', a woman priest, said the mere fact of her speaking out had damaged her prospects of a career in the church. Nor does she have a great deal of confidence in the new system.

'If a parishioner came to me now, there's a hell of a lot we could do to make a difference, but to go through official church channels, it's not something I would have a lot of faith in.'

She said she was still coming across women who had offered themselves for ordination but dropped out because of sexual harassment.

Helen said the complaints laid by her and other women never went to a formal hearing because church officials believed that alleged behaviour did not take place within a two-year time limit set down by church law. However, another complainant said no-one checked with her and the abuse had occurred within the deadline.

Helen said the clergyman undertook to write a letter expressing regret for his behaviour and acknowledging it was not the fault of the women. This never happened.

He resigned after his employers were made aware of the complaints and he was formally admonished by the church. He lost a number of church posts, had to work under supervision, undertook to have therapy and was forbidden to work in any situation where he would supervise women alone.

Now a trained therapist, Ann says the clergyman took advantage of her vulnerability. 'I felt really unattractive, I didn't think anyone would want to have sexual contact with me and I really needed to be special.

'He was a very compelling man, a very charming man, very seductive and he was somebody I had shared the most intimate details of my life with.'

After she stopped going to him for counselling he turned up at her flat and demanded she have oral sex with him. 'Within two to three minutes it was over and he left without saying anything. It was awful.'

There were other incidents of physical harassment when he visited her at work. After a long battle the Accident Compensation Corporation accepted an abuse claim and she used the $7500 payment for further therapy.

In a letter to the archbishop, Ann said the clergyman's misconduct had seriously affected her self-esteem, caused sexual difficulties in her marriage and eroded her faith. 'I didn't go to church for a long time and I changed denominations. I thought if this is what goes on with people who represent the church, then what is the church about?'

'Pat' had a similar experience to Ann when she went to the clergyman for informal counselling in her late teens. Later she had dealings with him through her job and she again experienced sexual harassment. 'He's an extremely powerful man and he was a person I really feared to make an enemy of, because that whole side of him was not known to other people.'

'Jo', now an ordained priest, said she rejected the clergyman's physical advances, so he appealed to her for sympathy over his marital problems. 'I was put in the situation of being the caring nurturing young mother who could deal with all these things.'

He began ringing two and three times a day, saying he loved her and visiting her home unexpectedly. She said he raped her twice and she considered laying a criminal complaint, but decided it would be the end of her marriage and would be devastating for her children.

'I was able to identify what was happening when I started reading the court pages in the newspaper. I saw people doing things like this were being tried in the courts and sentenced to imprisonment.'

Scared of jeopardising her career in the church, she kept the problem secret till after her ordination. 'For me, it felt as if I was fighting a cosmic battle between good and evil. He did it to a lot of people and we all protected him because he was such a dear man, and so kind and so good, and no-one was going to give him away.'

After laying the complaint she said she was made to feel like a prostitute and received abusive telephone calls from other women priests.

Archbishop D confirmed that a group of women visited him to discuss the sexual harassment allegations made about the clergyman. He said the church did not try to brush the matter under the carpet. 'It was not a whitewash, because the person and his wife suffered tremendously because of the action taken by the church against him.'

The archbishop said the women concerned had a lot of support within the diocese concerned. 'I honestly don't think there was a witch hunt, I think that some people felt that the women went over the top in some respects in terms of emphasising the punishment side too much and not allowing room for repentance, forgiveness and restoration.'

Archbishop D suggested the women had sinned by discussing the outcome of the confidential meeting with him. He also disputed the rape claim. 'We have heard both sides of the story, and I still would find it really hard to describe what happened as rape. It takes two to tango and, sometimes, as in this case, no doubt a person who was in a position of power and authority misused that, but to then go and say that what happened in a particular instance was rape is, I think, stretching things.'

Archbishop D says he was not happy with the way the case was handled, but he felt the women had to bear some of the responsibility for their failure to report the problem sooner. 'It's just beyond my comprehension. If it was such a bad experience from the women's point of view, why did they go back for more?'

The fact that the women regarded the clergyman as an influential member of the church hierarchy was not a sufficient explanation. 'For this to be allowed to continue with so many women, I really find it hard to understand.'

He said there had not been any talk of relicencing the clergyman but he could not rule that out completely in the future.

Archbishop D said that since his ordination in 1960 he had heard of only one other case of sexual harassment. 'It's not rampant and it would be quite irresponsible to suggest that. It's certainly not a major issue for the church in the sense that major numbers of clergy are suddenly misbehaving.'

Earlier this year Anglican vicar Jenny Dawson was a keynote speaker at a Christchurch forum on sexual abuse by clergy and she believes this sort of unethical conduct is rife.

She says male ministers are in a very powerful position. They often have ready access to parishioners' homes, and are trusted by women seeking spiritual guidance or counselling. To her the power imbalance makes sexual relationships between clergy and parishioners totally unacceptable, and she says they cannot just be passed off as 'affairs'. Many clergy do not have professional supervisors to oversee their counselling work, largely because of the cost.

In 1990 Anglican priest and marriage guidance counsellor Ken Davy said clergy who sexually abused their clients tended to be

> lonely men who repressed their own problems and sought healing through relationships with parishioners.
>
> When the *Dominion Sunday Times* approached him for this article he said he was not allowed to comment further to the media, but another source provided a copy of a 1990 paper Mr Davy had written about sexual entanglements between clergy and parishioners.
>
> In it he said sexual assaults by pastors occurred more or less regularly, and gave five examples of offending clergy from various denominations. In one of the case studies a woman ended up in a relationship with a minister after going to him for marriage guidance. She confided in another minister but he advised her to tell no-one. She later discovered this had happened in other parishes and the offending pastor had merely been admonished and moved on.
>
> Mr Davy said efforts by church authorities to hush up sexual abuse by clergy deterred victims from seeking help and effectively branded them as lepers. He concluded that pastors who repeatedly abused women had an addiction which was more powerful than alcoholism and he doubted that they could ever be trusted within the church again.

In the *Dominion Sunday Times* of 24 May 1992, in a letter to the editor, the letter writer commented about how 'saddened and maddened' she was by the archbishop's attitude to sexual abuse within the Anglican Church.

> I was saddened because once again women are being made scapegoats for sexual abuse, and maddened because once again the same old hoary justifications about the reasons for abuse were trotted out.
>
> The comment by the archbishop that the women had sinned by

> discussing publicly what happened is to imply that it is to their shame that it happened. If he believes the women are blameless, why should they not be open and honest? Or does he subscribe to the fantasy that all women really 'want it' anyway.
>
> As for the women concerned 'going over the top' in emphasising punishment instead of forgiveness and restoration, how much more would my faith have been strengthened if the church hierarchy had gone 'over the top' in protecting women from the likelihood of physical, emotional and sexual abuse happening within the church again.
>
> I find it inconceivable that Archbishop D does not have any knowledge of the ideologies in a patriarchal society that keep women in a violent relationship.
>
> I suggest to a church that tells us 'love thy neighbour' that it adds, 'and recognise thy women as equal'.

In that same paper, under a headline 'College silent on sex case', an article, again written by Amanda Cropp, disclosed the name of the offender. When interviewed, the principal at Palmerston North's International Pacific College, a private college for overseas students, refused to comment on claims that a clergyman employed by the college was disciplined by the Anglican Church in 1989 after allegations of sexual harassment. He would not say whether he knew before R's appointment as provost about the allegations and action taken by the church, saying that it was an ecclesiastical matter and the allegations had no relevance to R's performance of his duties.

R was also asked for an interview, but he referred the *Dominion Sunday Times* to his lawyer, who also refused to comment. The article summarised the events beginning with the complaints received by the bishop in September 1989, and listed the positions held at the time by R, including his involvement in producing the revised New Zealand Prayer Book. It quoted from a letter written to the women complainants by the bishop in October 1989 which stated that the church took seriously any allegations of sexual harassment or misconduct. The bishop's letter had said that complaints about R, though unspecific in some cases and unsubstantiated in others, had been investigated, that R had been admonished formally and had had seniority removed. He was not permitted to stand for General Synod and was no longer an examining chaplain, no longer involved with post-ordination training, had been replaced on the Provincial Board of Ministry and on Theological Education by Extension. There would be no situation in which he would supervise a woman alone. He had begun regular therapy and was to continue in therapy to ensure attitudes were carefully monitored. He was required to be in supervision and had been removed from training roles except in group situations in a limited role when called in by someone else.

The bishop was also interviewed and told the *Dominion Sunday Times* that he did not write R a reference for his position at the International Pacific College and did not know about the job until after R had left Christchurch. When the *Dominion Sunday Times* began asking church sources about the allegations, R's lawyers wrote to the paper requesting that no article be published on the grounds that the interpretation of events reported to the newspaper were questionable and pointed out the significance of the fact that no action had been taken through civil or criminal courts and the matter did not go before a church tribunal.

We were interested to note the refusal to comment by most of those interviewed and the stance taken by the church that it was enough to have deprived R of his ecclesiastical positions and offered him counselling. We were most interested in comments made by R's lawyers to the end that it was the women's integrity and honesty that was questionable, not his, which was verified by the fact that no action had been taken by the women through the civil or criminal courts. The article did not add that the archbishop had forbidden us access to the public legal system, saying that as members of the church we were under the law of the church, the law of forgiveness and reconciliation.

✣

The matter took an interesting turn when the *Dominion Sunday Times* of 11 October 1992 published an editorial by John Kennedy about the Roman Catholic priest in Gore who had abused several boys. Kennedy said that the case should have been dealt with by the police rather than the church and the school, and that the secrecy that surrounded the handling of the problem caused public scandal and outrage, which prevented the priest from having a fair trial. He said that the church lost credibility with the community and left people to assume that the clergy are above the law or else they enjoy special protection. He said that the priest should be returned to New Zealand for trial instead of being whisked off overseas out of harm's way. Referring to an Irish Roman Catholic bishop who had fathered a child, he said that many Catholics were more critical of the woman than of the bishop because she could have insisted on him meeting his parental obligations without making it public.

Kennedy wished the Anglicans well in their re-examination of its attitudes and teachings about sexuality, which he declared to be one of the most difficult issues of our time, especially since traditional moral values no longer hold across large sections of our community. He said that many women in the Roman Catholic Church feel that they are discriminated against and want to be properly represented in the church's decision-making structures. The women claim that their talents are seriously under-used and that the development of their skills is blocked by 'pre-conceived stereo-typing' and 'gender restrictions'. He concluded that many parish priests lack the ability to communicate or relate to women effectively and that the church's traditional view of women as mothers and homemakers is too limiting. He said that religious organisations have the desire to handle their ethical problems far away from the public eye and are not obligated to reveal their ethical codes and disciplinary procedures. Kennedy concluded that most religious groups do not like to draw attention to the fact that sexual misconduct by their clergy even takes place, so they are not motivated towards generating public statements concerning this problem.

The Roman Catholic Church offers the excuse of celibacy for why its priests abuse children. They say that during training celibacy is discussed openly, but that does not stop them from struggling with the deprivation of one of their strongest and most driving powers, their sexuality. No one has offered an explanation or excuse for why priests and ministers in other denominations, those which allow marriage, inflict the same sexual pressures on those under their care.

On 29 September 1994, *The Press* published an article about a group of Catholic women in Wellington who wanted churches to disclose the names of religious abusers to their congregations. The Susanna Group complained to the Wellington Catholic Archdiocese that its draft guidelines allowed abusers to hide under confidentiality that protected the abuser from openly accepting responsibility and left the community without protection against future abuse. The guidelines talked of safeguarding reputations and avoiding the risk of scandal, a policy which the group saw as covert collusion, whether consciously or unconsciously so. The Anglican Archbishop D was asked to comment about the issue of removing confidentiality from an abuser. He replied that his diocese had not addressed this and added: 'But the church network is pretty effective. When someone has misbehaved and their licence has been removed, word soon gets around.' He was more prepared for the gossip machine to do his work for him than to have an open and honest communication with church members to reveal the name of the offender. This is a spurious way to allow the church to operate. Speculation and rumour can do more to destroy reputations and make the scandal that much more scandalous than if the church had a policy of those much preached-about ethical commodities called truth and honesty. When people are given correct and factual information, scandal is less likely to happen and reputations are more likely to be saved.

In *The Press* of 3 December 1994, in an article reprinted from the *Independent*, it was said that in 1992 the Roman Catholic Church had expressed the concern that 'priests' sexual abuse of children and adolescents and sexual misconduct is the most serious problem we in the church have faced in centuries'. Others say that the problem has been hidden for a long time and is finally being talked about. When a problem of sexual abuse or misconduct surfaced in a parish the priest would be moved to another parish, thus spreading the problem and allowing more people to be damaged by the offender. It seems that the church's response has been to protect itself and its priests rather than to protect potential victims by the use of common law. The Catholic Church in Ireland simply sees itself outside the law in these and other matters. Even when the law is invoked by others, the common expectation in Ireland is that the church will employ levers in high places to mitigate the damage. The article continued, saying that the Roman Catholic Church cannot continue to hide what has happened. The church has to reconsider its influence over people's lives and, at the very least, the church's position as a force for conservatism is now in question. The church is a society within a society. Priests have tended to be free of the moral constraints that ordinary mortals have to contend with. The church should stop unctuous moralising from the pulpit. The church has been shaken to its foundations and if it wants to maintain its power and respect it has to do some hard image rebuilding. No one is going to abolish the church, but part of its authority has been chipped away.

✣

Why the secrecy? Why does every denomination run for cover and prevent the truth from emerging? Why do women victims of this abuse keep silent even though they know that it is ultimately destructive? Rutter has attempted to explain this phenomenon of secrecy and find a reason why this abuse has been kept hidden for so long. He posits the theory that lying has become an acceptable mode in male-dominated institutions where truth is often the victim of political considerations. The suppression of truth is seen as necessary to preserve order, and institutions exist to maintain the order of the status quo. All its systems are geared up for this maintenance and anything that emerges to disrupt the status quo is hastily pushed out of sight so that the reputation of the institution is protected and preserved. The institution of the church has more at stake than most other institutions, since it exists on the charitable donations of people who believe that the church stands holy and sacred in an ungodly world. Thus it has more to lose in terms of reputation and status. By denying the existence of immorality within its own ranks, the church increases the protection of those who use this denial to exploit the very people who need the care and the nurture of the church for their own growth towards wholeness.

Another factor in the suppression of information about sexually deviant priests lies within the dictum of the church, which says 'Judge not lest you be judged'. This could be another reason why religious organisations simply transfer clergy to other parishes with no public admission of misconduct. We all sin, if not in action, at least in thought. 'There but for the grace of God go I' is perhaps allied to the instruction not to judge others.

I encountered this sentiment when I served as a councillor on a district council. A teacher in a small country school was found to have sexually abused some of his pupils. He was sentenced to 100 hours of community work and was put in charge of the children's section of the public library. Many parents objected that he was being punished in an environment where he could re-offend. As the councillors, mostly male, debated his position, a vote was taken and the majority agreed that he should remain in the library in the children's section on the grounds that he had suffered enough. Yet his suffering was minimal compared with the untold suffering that he had caused his victims, who were small children under his care. Underneath this apparent forgiveness for unforgivable sexual abuse lay the feeling 'It could have been me, therefore who am I to judge'. The person who accompanied this teacher to plead for his reinstatement was the vicar of the local Anglican church.

FIVE

Reflections

At the same time that we were struggling to understand what was happening to us, several books were being prepared for publication on the subject of sexual abuse in a professional relationship based on trust. Marie Fortune published her book *Is Nothing Sacred? The Story of a Pastor, the Women He Sexually Abused, and the Congregation He Nearly Destroyed* (Harper) in 1989 in America. At the same time, Dr Peter Rutter published his book *Sex in the Forbidden Zone* in 1989, also in America. He found, as I had, that there was very little literature published on sexual abuse in professional relationships based on trust. The only mention that I had ever found was a small piece in Gail Sheehy's book *Passages* (Bantam Books, 1977) where she talks briefly about relationships between students and their teachers. Neither could Rutter find any published statistical study of sexual misconduct among clergymen, even though evidence has it that the incidence among male clergymen is higher than the ten per cent estimated for male psychotherapists.

These books offered situational evidence of the existence of the problem in other parts of the world and confirmed for us that we were not struggling with a marshmallow monster but with a real problem for women that had, up until this time, never been talked about openly. They offered a sound analysis of the general behaviour and the cultural values that enabled this form of misuse of power to occur. What Rutter offered in particular was a generalised answer to the question on everyone's lips: 'Why do men do it and why do women consent?' It was helpful to know that we were not alone in our struggles and that we were not inventing the problem.

Why do men do it?

Dr Peter Rutter offers a professional understanding of the men who use their power to sexually abuse women. It is helpful for women to understand why men engage in this practice, because knowledge itself is power. If women know the traps that are hidden within these relationships then the potential for exploitation and sexual victimisation can be defused. Women who do experience this behaviour can recognise it and report it to the person who has been nominated by the institution to instigate the complaint process. It is to be hoped that reporting this will not damage the women's future career. The following is a summary of Rutter's findings.

He says that the way men in power exploit a woman's trust seems to be virtually identical whether the man is a doctor, psychiatrist, psychologist, therapist, professor, mentor, priest or minister. As more women enter the professional workplace the problem of sex between mentor and protégée becomes increasingly prevalent in a relationship that is unequal in terms of power.

On a broad social level our culture encourages men to push against women's sexual boundaries, especially in relationships of unequal power founded on trust. As well as this, it is instilled in our culture that a man's word is always believed over and against the word of a woman who challenges him. On a professional level, the men who have power over women are often those who have chosen to help others as their life's work. They are usually talented men and are always considered to be outstanding members of their profession.

The long term underlying psychological patterns that make men vulnerable to their own sexual impulses are threefold. First, success itself puts men at a higher level of risk of exploiting women sexually because they believe that they are above normal ethical demands and think that they can make their own rules. Second, chronic depression can be an occupational hazard in these type of professions and they conceal this depression behind their position of power; then, in order to keep functioning in their jobs, they create a sexual dynamic in the relationship with women in their care, who are ethically forbidden to them. Third, the lure of the forbidden draws men to want sex with women they are supposed to protect.

By using women sexually to sustain their positions of power, these men access vast resources of life-enhancing vitality and sexually generated energy. They feel alive as they emotionally feed off their women victims. Their claim of true love is spurious because it is self-serving and geared to sexual conquest. Their life, their fortune and their honour are put at risk for a few stolen moments. This type of self-serving sex is destructive to everyone concerned. While they are engaged on their mission of sexual conquest, men lose the ability to perceive how they hurt others. They may lose control and engage in violent or addictive behaviour. Psychologically speaking, the man has not only raped the woman but has committed an act of incest because of the nature of his power over her. Ultimately, the men can lose their families, their friends and their livelihoods. There are a few cold and amoral men who, by their habitual violation of women, could be labelled evil or sociopathic. Male victimisers try to evade responsibility by blaming their victims.

In the context of the church, where more women are seeking ordination, the position of mentor means that the teacher has a special responsibility for the ordinand. An important one-to-one relationship must develop between the man who is in charge of the woman's training and the woman under his care as he takes on the roles of teacher, confessor and guide. This man, who is in a position of power over a woman, holds a sacred trust to guard her welfare and to guide her safely into the church. He takes on a role of parent in his position of trust and authority and is charged with the ethical responsibilities of the parenting role.

Rutter's findings are an invaluable aid towards understanding this particular form of abuse. It is interesting to see how R fitted into this psychological analysis. R was very successful in the church, holding positions of seniority in the church hierarchy, but he was not paid by the church. His paid position was as the principal of a male university hostel. The culture of this position was ambiguous in that the college had been a theological college where priests were trained. That part of the college's function had shifted to Auckland some years ago, but because the college remained under the auspices of the Anglican Church, the college was still required to employ a priest as principal. Added to this requirement was the existence of the chapel and a good theological library within the grounds of the college. R took it upon himself to revive the college as a training and theological centre. These alternative activities were condoned and accepted by the board of governors, who allowed space at the college for theological education and regular ministerial training.

Because of his charisma—because he was funny, charming, clever and gossipy—R was surrounded by women who loved him. Older women adored him and went to him in the early evening to have a sherry and a chat. He had close friendships with these women but he did not sexually pursue them. When the crisis broke, these women were his main supporters and the chief antagonists of the women who submitted complaints about his inappropriate behaviour. For his sexual satisfactions he chose younger women with some outstanding physical characteristic who were either working under him or who had been consigned to his care. Very often they were mothers with young children.

R was the keeper of the gate into the church. Those who put themselves forward as candidates for ordination were sent to him first for a preliminary assessment. As an examining chaplain he was in a position to select ordinands for training. The women who put themselves forward as candidates placed their own future careers in the church in R's hands, and invested a lot of hope and trust in him. Once they had passed through the selection process, R was in charge of all their training, pre-ordination as well as post-ordination, pastoral and theological. The only way that he could sustain this workload was to tap into the sexual and spiritual energies of women. By and large women gave him everything he needed, and when they did not give it freely, he took it from them by force.

This was not difficult for R to do, since he was trained to manipulate people's emotions. My guess is that he was influenced by the sexual revolution of the sixties and seventies, when women's sexuality was put under the microscope by Kinsey, Masters and Johnson, and Shere Hite and these investigators declared that women were now free from sexual inhibitions. Shere Hite in particular distinguished women's sexual needs as separate and independent from men's sexual needs. This separation of the sexual needs of women from the sexual needs of men was a new phenomenon and outlined the beginnings of a sexual revolution where it was ascertained that women did not exist simply to service men's sexual needs. This new independence offered to women the opportunity to take control over their own bodies and their own sexual needs and brought about a release from the ancient social taboos that governed women's behaviour.

This is about the time that R, as far as we can ascertain, began to engage sexually with women in his care as part of their 'therapy'. He seemed to assume that all women were sexually liberated and, if they were not, then he would teach them how to be sexually liberated with him if they were privileged enough to have been chosen by him. He was acutely aware through his counselling work that the social structures that had been kept in place for years to protect women from 'red-blooded males' had been torn down to reveal that women are not passive vehicles for men's pleasure and that they too had their own sexual desires and fantasies. Contraception enabled women to be responsible for their own bodies and offered them the freedom to choose their partners. All he had to do was to tap into women's emotions and he knew that the rest was easy. The fear of making a woman pregnant, the great taboo that had hitherto protected women from the rampant sexuality of men, had been erased; so women were confronted with their own sexuality in a way that had never happened before. In R's mind therefore, there was no reason why a woman should not freely engage in sexual activities in the same way he did. The only barrier remaining for complete sexual freedom was the individual's moral code of commitment, loyalty and fidelity.

As well as these areas of disengagement from tradition, the church began to follow the ideological movement of radical freedom. The post-war messages of individualism opened the way to free the individual from the trammels of cultural mores. These were bound to include freedom from sexual taboos, a freedom that would release women from their enculturated passivity. Feminist theologians began to re-examine biblical texts from a perspective of radical suspicion, challenging the male dominated interpretations and searching the texts to liberate the women in the Bible from the chauvinistic attitude of writers and interpreters, to offer them an identity of their own and an understanding of their condition so long ago in history. It is important to note that many of the women mentioned in both the old and new testaments are present in the text because they are judged by their sexuality and considered to be sinners or 'fallen women'. A new theology for women emerged from their labours, a new freedom and a new equality in the church. Women began to take their rightful place in an institution that had hitherto excluded them on the grounds that they were sub-human. There was a simultaneous movement towards the ordination of women. R was involved in this and he was a strong advocate for women's ministry. Feminism became a cultural and a spiritual revolution. Every facet of the Bible and biblical teaching was overturned like the tables in the temple. Feminists wanted equality in the church. But I did not know all this. During that time I was busy bringing up my children in the country and struggling to cope with the traditional expectations imposed on rural women.

R's price for his support of churchwomen for ordination was high. On a personal level he found he had a readily available source of energy, so grateful were women to him for his encouragement and his endorsement of their spirituality. Women were a ready source of nurture and compassion for him and also provided creative ideas, which he used as his own without acknowledging their source. He twisted the moral teachings of the church for his own ends. His belief that the act of adultery meant vaginal sex was a self-justification for his sexual acts: any other sexual activity he did not classify as adultery. Thus he considered himself free to engage in any other form of sexual activity, without sin. In his mind, women existed for his own sexual purposes, and these purposes he believed were biblically not sinful. When I asked him how he could commit adultery with so many women and then stand in the pulpit to preach about morality, he replied that he did not preach about morality. In his mind, avoiding preaching about any moral issues exonerated him from sin, even though he worked in an institution that stands for morality.

Although R gained creative energy and ideas from his sexual victims, they were not counted as his friends. They were carefully kept hidden so that he could carry out his public duties. He could not afford to carry his seedy private life into his public life by inviting his private friends along with his public friends. He ruthlessly used the energy gained from his private life to maintain his public life and never mixed the two. It was inconvenient to him if his private life overlapped his public one. He bound the women who were part of his private life into secrecy by telling all his women victims that he loved them. R knew that the mere word 'love' binds a woman into a complicity with a man, into an intimacy that no other word can deliver. As soon as the word love is used, a woman is hooked, either positively or negatively, and becomes a source of energy. R was addicted to sex as other people are addicted to alcohol or drugs. His need for sex rendered him oblivious to the needs of the women on whom he preyed as he ruthlessly sought to fulfil his own addictive needs. His addiction rendered him manic at times, sending him off on a sexual rampage. He became careless in the end, when his addiction finally overcame his sense of social restraint. He fell amongst the ranks of sociopaths who have incurable sexual urges.

Why do women consent?

Many people have expressed bewilderment about why a woman consents in these circumstances. It is hard for anyone who does not understand the nature of power to comprehend why a mature woman can allow such a detrimental relationship to develop.

Dr Peter Rutter has attempted to answer this difficult question from a psychological point of view. He says that it is important to understand that these relationships offer the woman immeasurable value in terms of hope and offer them access to their deepest resources of self. A woman can adore a man who offers her such hope, but this is not sexual. It is more likely to be similar to the love for a parent, since she is looking for his recognition of her as an individual. She may want to emulate him, become like him in terms of strength and competence, but being his sexual partner is the last thing on her mind. But women have discovered that few relationships with men are safe from sexual demands, and if this relationship is important, the woman has to choose either to overlook the sexual demands or respond to them if she is not to lose a relationship of value to her. Because the man so often controls the woman's access to her future, the man's insistence upon his sexuality becomes a barrier to the woman's development. If she does yield or make any compromise she gives up control over her intimate boundaries and becomes a victim. Then she has no other choice but to trust that the man will use his power to help her rather than to exploit her.

Rutter says that ultimately a woman has no option but to allow herself to be sexually exploited because the dynamics of the forbidden zone render her unable to withhold consent.

Psychologically, she is not free to say yes or no. When she experiences sexual touching she feels danger and experiences paralysis of action, judgement, feeling and voice. When she first perceives that her mentor is improperly sexualising a relationship, her physical experiences can be nausea, muscle tension or trembling as well as emotional feelings of dread, anxiety, depression or blackness. She finds that she has no boundaries with which to protect herself because she is bereft of self; she discovers that she has no power, no control and no choice. What she does experience, in fact, is the psychic numbing of a post-traumatic stress disorder. She feels no physical pleasure because her inner self recognises her danger and permits her body little or no pleasure. Instead she experiences real pain and nausea or feelings of numbness and deadness. She has a powerful ambivalence in her conflict between participation and revulsion. At the very moment that an exploitative sexual relationship begins, she is nauseated, sickened, repulsed, and degraded.

Often the woman has forgotten her sense of self, especially if she is busy looking after children or parents, so she is unable to find the voice to say no when she is sexually invaded. The man is in a position to free her from the limitations imposed by her family and to bring the woman back to the life of the mind and offer her hope for a life in the outside world. But he demands the high price of her spirit or body or both, and instead of providing freedom and life he leads the woman totally away from herself and uses her for himself without tenderness or consideration for her feelings. The subsequent damage is similar to that of rape or incest. The woman turns the feeling of revulsion against herself. She is unable to understand how fully she has been victimised and she turns the blame and subsequent self-hatred on herself. The most critical damage is in the silencing of her own voice and the violation of her sense of self. Any sexual behaviour by a man in power within the forbidden zone is inherently exploitative of a woman's trust, her spirit, her sexuality and her capacity for compassion.

But women have tended not to act on these feelings. Rutter explains that women go against their deepest feelings because force is being applied to them emotionally if not physically, especially if the relationship has a parent-child quality to it. When children feel unloved and abandoned they will do anything to win back the love of their parents, no matter how much abuse they have suffered; in the same way the woman in this situation will attempt to heal the man who has abused her.

Most women did not know there were ethical standards, and in some situations criminal laws, that prohibited such involvement. It is now commonly acknowledged that the laws that define professional malpractice recognise that the man can exercise a life-and-death power over the woman. Victims do not report sexual assault with a man in a professional relationship because they are subjected to further humiliation and brutalisation as they try to enlist the aid of authorities in bringing their victimisers to justice. The legal system has a well-deserved reputation for not responding to women's complaints of sexual exploitation by men. Most women would rather absorb their injury privately than risk the ordeal of a public battle in which they are likely to become targets for the deeply held 'blame the victim' attitudes so prevalent in our culture. Most women never speak out about exploitative sex, and those who do may have to fight a nearly impossible uphill battle against public shame, the statute of limitations, burdens of proof, procedural and bureaucratic nightmares and masculine tendency toward mutual protection that discredits and blames women who bring such charges. Thus an enforced, complex, psychological and cultural silence is observed by the woman, and also by witnesses who do nothing to stop it. The reality of the social environment is that men have until now been able to get away with sexual violations, and sexual exploitation has been a low-risk behaviour.

Rutter concludes that the damage caused by the betrayal of intimate trust is severe. The feminine turns against itself, telling the woman that she is a liability in the workplace, the political arena and in public life. She is robbed of the best years of her life, which are spent sunk in this black mire. She has been overcome by evil from which she may or may not be able to disengage. Finally, she begins to believe in the cultural message of female passivity.

The need for secrecy

Rutter talks about the enforced and complex psychological and cultural silence that is observed by the woman in this situation. This aspect held great fascination for me because I had struggled to make sense of my own position at the time, and I can quite understand the dilemma of the archbishop when he publicly stated that he could not understand why women consented to this sexual activity if they did not think it was right, and why they did not report it until a long time afterwards. I emerged from the deep abyss with some insight into the dilemma of women when confronted with this conundrum. It is my belief that the system of values that underpins our culture contributes significantly to women's consent.

Rutter offers some insight into the need for secrecy. He suspects that there is a conspiracy of silence among men in the helping professions to the extent that the professional bodies concerned refuse to fund any research into men's sexually predatory behaviour. He outlines the reasons why the suppression mirrors the secrecy that is urged on the victims, and emphasises the importance of breaking the silence in defiance of the code of secrecy.

The reasons for this suppression is that some men hope they will be able to have sex with someone in their care, and that if they do not they would like to and do not want to stop other men from having sexual relations with women in their care. These men need help and seek inappropriate ways to find it, believing that their healing lies in having sexual contact with a woman. So long as they believe that, they will not stop their predatory behaviour.

They are confident in the knowledge that women will not mention an exploitative sexual relationship to anyone at all and certainly not to anyone who has disciplinary authority over a man in power.

Suppression of the truth is seen to be necessary to preserve order in any institution, and, as a consequence, lying becomes an acceptable behaviour on personal and eventually national and global levels, especially in the political arena. This is reflected in the way male-dominated institutions deal with sexual misconduct by their own members, where truth is often a victim of political considerations. There exists a fear that the reputation of the profession itself will be damaged. The institution of the church has more to lose in these terms than secular institutions, since it occupies a self-imposed high moral ground in our culture with its teaching and preaching about right living, therefore it must lie by denying that it employs sexual deviants who break its own moral code. This ethical conundrum is compounded by economic necessity, since the church is dependent for its existence on the voluntary donations of money by its members. When the church falls into disrepute, the offertory diminishes in proportion. So it is easy to understand that religious organisations desire to handle their ethical problems far away from the public eye. Neither is the church obligated to reveal its ethical codes and disciplinary procedures. Most religious groups do not like to draw attention to the fact that sexual misconduct by their clergy even takes place so they are not motivated toward generating public statements concerning this problem.

Without the truth we become helpless to change anything in our lives and in our world. Rutter says that the church, in these situations, is given an opportunity to enhance its reputation by taking a position of honesty about its unethical members, and if the institution does not take this opportunity freely and voluntarily, then it will be forced into it by public pressure or new legislation. Other sources have commented on the church's inability to deal with situations in which their priests or ministers exploit the vulnerable people in their care. We have read with horror the stories about the way in which religious organisations transfer their sexually abusive clergy to other parishes without making a public admission of misconduct, even though they know that most men who have sexually exploited women or children are likely to continue doing so in future positions of power.

Obedience

Our value system tells us what is good behaviour and what is not. Values exist to keep a culture structured and orderly by modifying human behaviour. When we examine these designer-living values we can see that they are quite coercive in nature, and this coercion gives us information about the constitution of our culture. One of the best ways of telling when a violation of cultural values has occurred is when an offender is punished for not adhering to community rules. When behaviour does not meet up with the value, coercion is applied to turn that behaviour around to what is deemed good by that community. For example, disobedience is punished, but obedience is not rewarded. We can assume then that obedience is an expected and normal behaviour.

But there is more to a value than meets the eye. For many years I wrestled with obedience. I have a reasonable idea of what obedience is, since I was frequently punished as a child for disobedience. But obedience is not very attractive in our culture today, and it is interesting to note that the vow by a wife to obey her husband has been removed from the marriage service. When I asked some friends what they thought about obedience, one said, 'Oh, I'm sorry but you are asking the wrong person. I am a specialist in disobedience. Obedience is way out of line for me.' Her chosen role is to question government policies by talking to the people who are disadvantaged by them, and then to make television documentaries about them. She uses her finely honed disobedience as a tool for social justice, to ensure that the powerful do not ride roughshod over the powerless. She is the voice of the powerless to ensure that democracy and social policy combine for the good of all people. I am grateful for her disobedience. She is not blindly obedient to the world as it is, but is obedient to her vision of the world as it could be. In her disobedience there lies a spirituality of a future hope that can be realised.

My second friend, who is a struggling writer with four children, says that obedience does not enter her vocabulary. She says she is not so much obedient to an external voice as she is obedient to her own values and her own talents. She has a wonderful sense of self, which flows out freely to others, because she is obedient to her own inner self and she expects others to be true to their own inner prompting.

When I ask my sister what she understands by obedience, she tells me to 'f… off'. Coarse language is uncharacteristic for her, so I am shocked by the violence of her reaction. Rather pedantically, I am forced to interpret her violent expletive as saying that obedience for her is anathema, a curse, a violation of her innermost being. I understand her reply to mean that obedience would cause her to stop doing that which is most important to her and which she has struggled against all odds to achieve. She has stepped out of the narrow confines of obedience to social conformity and has chosen her own path in life, which is to be a great artist. The sacrifices for her have been immense. She has had to leave her own country and live overseas away from her family in order to be successful. She guards her territory jealously.

These words of defiance cause me to believe that obedience is a huge issue for women. Against what exactly are these women rebelling? What expectations have been demanded of them in the past that have led them to this decision not to obey? It would appear from this admittedly small but significant sample of women who are achievers that my friends are afraid of something.

They are afraid of conforming to the great ideal of womanhood, which takes many forms—the virgin woman, the sexual woman and the wife-and-mother woman; afraid of being condemned socially for not conforming to the standard laid down in culture; afraid for their own talents, about which they are passionate and focused in order to protect them.

And yet at the same time that they are unutterably true to themselves, they see themselves as being disobedient. They see that they are at odds with what they consider to be the normal code of behaviour for women. What is this normal code of behaviour for women, and who has laid this down as a path for women to follow? I think it is important to explore the concept of obedience in order to discover what is so bad about this 'good' ethic.

The *Oxford Dictionary* says that to obey means to carry out a command, as in 'you will obey me', or to do what one is told to do. Obedience is the submission to another's rule or authority and compliance with a law or a command. The root of our English word comes from the Latin *audire*, to hear. Hebrew also uses the verb to hear, *shama*, as the base for obedience, as does Greek. A verbal command from a person in authority is heard by another in an inferior position either by choice, vocational expectation or social position. The emphasis is on the spoken word as a command as it is heard by another. Some sources say that obedience is an ethic, but my dictionary of ethics does not include obedience. If obedience is not an ethic, then it is difficult to put it into a category. If it is a value, then all people should be obedient. If it is a moral, then disobedience is immoral.

From the dictionary definition it would seem that obedience is a verbal transaction between two parties, the one who gives the verbal command and the other who hears it and acts upon it. What is not stated within the definition is the intellectual and moral decision of the person who is the recipient of the verbal command. Obedience is not a natural reaction to a command.

The hearer has to weigh up the desirability of the command and then make a decision whether to obey or to disobey.

We are all aware that obedience in some things is desirable for survival, as for instance the obedience of children to their parents for their security, obedience to the road code for safety, obedience to the commandments not to kill or to steal so we can live peacefully together in our community. But blind obedience without the inner workings of moral and intellectual assent to an external authority is foolish and dangerous. Apart from the abdication of autonomy, the handing over of personal power to an impersonal authority can lead to a dangerous autocracy. Absolute power in the hands of a few can lead to all sorts of terrible inflictions upon those who have surrendered their personal power. The process of moral and intellectual assent allows an individual to weigh up the good or bad inherent within the command. Without this intellectual and moral assent to a command, authoritarianism is given absolute power, with the consequences that history relates. Often this inner moral and intellectual assent to those in power is compromised by the promise of money, a fulfilment of ambition, a need for security or a desire to please combined with the thought: What's in it for me?

Obedience is thus bipolar in terms of good and bad. On the one hand it is good when it is applied for survival, security and the physical and moral health and well-being of any group of people who live together in community. On the other hand, obedience is bad when the individual is required to forsake her or his right to intellectual and moral assent and therefore autonomy. The result is that individual power is sacrificed to the one who demands obedience, and this person gathers up the collective power and uses the individuals as tools to create more power. Individuals thus must deny access to their own intellectual or moral assent and give themselves over to the greater power, resulting in self-abnegation or the denial of the self for the greater good. There is an ambivalence between individual good and the community good. The community desires obedience from the individual for the good of the whole; but when the community overrides the assent of the individual, the result is evil because it destroys the individual.

Now we begin to see what it is exactly that women find so bad about obedience. The role of women in the community is seen to be to serve men. Women question this role, which has been culturally imposed upon them. Their intellect and moral conscience tells them that they do not like this imposed role. They do not give their intellectual and moral assent to conform to what they see as a patriarchal culture because, if they are obedient to its dictates, they must sacrifice their richest and deepest resource, their own self. In order to be true to this sense of self, they are forced into a position of disobedience in reaction against society's expectations that they will conform to the male vision of the ideal woman. This vision of the ideal woman has not been invented by women for women, but by men for men. Women are now reacting strongly against this vision of the ideal woman. They are disobedient to the constraints that it puts upon their freedom to be themselves in terms of their intellect, their creativity and their own values.

In spite of recent advances made by women, the culture that we have inherited and in which we live remains patriarchal, by which I mean that power, property and money largely belong to men. We accept this as a social norm. Society has absorbed the biblical message that women are inferior to men and must submit to men as their authority. It is only recently that women have attempted to redress the balance by saying that women are not inferior to men, only different; that women are fully human in spite of how men perceive them; and that women have the same legal rights as men.

However, the church has continued faithful to its ancient codes of practice, and only under duress has it heard the cries of women to be regarded as fully human. The scriptural passages that cause great distress to women are those written by Paul, who explains the cosmic pecking order in terms of God, men and then women who, because of their inferiority to men, must obey their husbands as their husbands must obey God. It is an extremely brilliant ploy to justify women's oppression by wrapping it up as a cosmic given and ordained by God. It is convenient for men to have women obey them and, when women buy into the scheme without intellectual or moral assent, it makes life very easy for men.

Personally, I find this cosmic pecking order pretty hard to take seriously and I think that men will go to any lengths in the attempt to enforce their superiority upon women. I have never felt that I was subhuman in any sense or that I ought to obey men. I have put the theory to the test and discovered through experience that my obedience to men only added fuel to their belief that they are superior to women and encouraged their autocracy. There still exists within our cultural norms an unresolved dichotomy between men's expectations of women and of themselves, and women's expectations of men and of themselves.

My experience of obedience followed a strange path. My response to what I sincerely believed to be a call from God to ordination was an act of obedience to that call. I did not fully understand it but I was willing to find out and put it to the test. I submitted to training for priesthood. At first I wanted to be obedient and to conform to whatever training programme had been scheduled for me by the church. Two bishops had requested that I train under R, and I wanted to train under him, so initially this did not pose a problem. The priesthood was still a new area of challenge for women and we were engaged in forging a path for women's full acceptance in the church. I did not want to rock the boat, not for myself, nor for any other women who were to enter the priesthood at any time. To my own surprise, I discovered that there were limits to my ability to be obedient to a regime I found to be sexually exploitative, manipulative and personally intrusive under the guise of 'spiritual training'. From the very first moment that I met R I could feel that he expected something, but I had no idea what it was. I felt uncomfortable and shook uncontrollably, which was unusual for me. Initially I attributed these feelings of unease to my nervousness at applying for ordination. I was excited about my selection for ordination, it was a privilege to have been chosen for this task and I felt very encouraged that the selection committee had deemed that I was a suitable candidate. From a personal point of view, however, I felt diffident about engaging with R because I was unclear at what level to engage. I had to leave that to him, since he was the professional, and I trusted him to guide me in what I thought would have been a spiritual journey.

Sex was the last thing on my mind. It came as a tremendous shock to discover that this was the level at which I was expected to engage with him. When these boundaries were violated by R's sexual advances I became very confused. It threw me into a mental chaos because it was so unexpected. Everything in my life turned upside down and I became very disoriented when my intellectual and moral assent was thrown off balance. What I believed to be wrong was said to be right and what I thought was right was wrong. I thought that perhaps this was to be the test of my obedience. Out of obedience I suppressed my intellect and my moral sense in order to observe what was happening. It opposed all that I had been taught by the church up until this time. It was an enigma.

R appeared to be much admired and loved by church people and he had a charismatic aura. I saw that he was surrounded by women, which struck me as odd in a male institution such as the college; it was also odd in the diocese, where the hierarchy was by and large male. The women that surrounded R were of two kinds. They were either mothers with young children or else they were older widows or spinsters. All the unsuspecting flies just buzzed into his office. He did not have to go out looking for us, we were sent to him like manna from heaven. The spider just waited in his web for us to come blundering along and fall through his office door. He was so addicted to women by the time I blundered in that I was just another one for the picking. We discovered later that he had been actively sexually engaged with women in his care for at least twenty years. There was no subtlety or careful preparation for a seduction. The church sent us to him for his feasts, and much later we were able to refer laughingly to the whitened bones of women outside his door. We women had no options, no choices and no existence for him apart from his desire to manipulate and exploit us.

R's greatest problem with me was that whereas he was quite single-minded about the reason for my presence in his office, I was equally single-minded about the reason for my presence in his office. The two were dissimilar. This conflict between sexuality and spirituality was to be my training for priesthood. I had undertaken a vocation that I considered to be holy and sacred in order to give a message to others about hope and love. In my mind this excluded sexuality. R had different ideas about that. And I was in his hands to guide me on this strange journey. If it had been the other way around and I was a person who was accustomed to making sexual advances to men, which I was not, as an ordinand it would still not have occurred to me to make sexual overtures to a man who was my spiritual guide into the church, even if I did feel any sexual attraction for him, which I did not. I did not need the burden of R's sexuality, having more than enough to keep me busy with all my domestic and community responsibilities.

At times, I did wonder whether perhaps this was an area of experience that R had identified for me for explore. It seemed to me to be a rather strange area of exploration for ordination, but he was my mentor and my guide and I had to decide whether I could trust him or not. I reasoned that if I could not trust him then there was little point in training with him; for if I was not able to trust him in this area of greatest vulnerability, then there was no way I could trust him in the equally vulnerable arena of spirituality. I made a decision to trust him, even though I knew this was an incredibly dangerous thing to do. By trusting him I was obeying the demands of the church, and therefore of God. If I had not obeyed him, I could not have trained for ordination. That was the deal. Obey R, obey the church, obey God. If I did not obey R, neither could I obey the church and ultimately I could not obey God. The equation was a bit extreme, but in the crisis of having to make a decision to obey, I could not think of any other way of thinking.

My intellectual freedom to assent or dissent was compromised to a degree that was emotionally and physically damaging. But at the same time that I suspended my intellectual and moral assent in order to be obedient, I discovered a truth about the place of women in the church and in society, and the truth about God. When a woman obeys the patriarchal vision of the ideal woman, she dies to her self. Obedience spells death to her intellect and her moral sense. When a woman disobeys the prevailing culture and church and takes a different path from the one that is laid down for her to follow, she will regain direct access to her intellect and her reason, her own morality, integrity, and creativity, and a new sense of being fully alive, fully human and fully aware of her place in the world.

The two most highly commended and admired acts of religious obedience in the Bible are those of Abraham and Jesus. Both of them involve the choice between life and death. Abraham's act of obedience to Yahweh was to kill his only son Isaac, who was the hope and promise of the future nation of Israel. In the end Yahweh relented, allowing Abraham to kill a ram instead of his son. Jesus, as the only son of God, was not so lucky. He was so obedient to God that he died one of the most painful deaths known to humanity. These two stories are hailed by the teaching of the church as the ultimate tests of obedience. The underlying message is that God is the ultimate authority over life and death, and that the command to die takes priority over the command to live. The ultimate test of obedience to God is to choose death over life. For a woman, this is absolutely contrary to her instinct to love life and to uphold the sacredness and blessedness of life.

As for me, this conflict between obedience and disobedience was a genuine struggle between life and death. The struggle was so hard that I was suicidal, choosing death over life. It took huge efforts—spiritually, emotionally, intellectually and physically—to conquer the idea of death and choose life. R led me so far away from myself that it was almost too difficult to find myself again.

Forgiveness

Another value that acts to cover up and condone acts of violence towards women lies deep within our set of cultural and spiritual values. The act of forgiveness is actively promoted by the dictum 'forgive and forget'. Forgiveness is seen as a good value because it restores peace. This is what forgiveness is all about. But there is an inherent process in the act of forgiveness, a process that must be carried out before forgiveness can be offered to an offender.

The biblical instruction for the process of forgiveness is written in Matthew 18:15–20. The first step towards forgiveness, after the injury has been inflicted, is for you, the victim, to go to the offender in order to discuss the offence. It seems only fair to confront the offending party first, in the hope that they can see that they have caused you injury. This offers a chance for the offender to defend him or herself and explain why he or she has hurt you. The offender may be angry about something else, or grieving, or be quite innocently unaware of the behaviour causing the offence. It is highly probable that the injury was not inflicted out of malice or even done intentionally. But it does need to be sorted out between the two of you so that each of you can clarify your own point of view and really listen to each other. The aim of this first encounter or confrontation is to resolve the conflict amicably. There is also an injunction in the text not to tell anyone else—this is a private matter between the two of you. This privacy protects both of you from public scorn. After all, you might have got the wrong end of the stick, and if it were made public you would feel foolish, or you would be forced into protecting your accusatory position, depriving the situation of flexibility. There is a possibility that the matter can be cleared up, that the person who has offended you will apologise and receive your forgiveness in return and reconciliation can be achieved.

If this private interview is not successful, all is not lost. You have another opportunity for forgiveness because the instructions insist that the issue not be abandoned or let lie. You can take one or two friends with you as support, people who can see both points of view, to a second interview, and mediate between the two of you. Although the offender remains unrepentant during a one-to-one confrontation, more voices in your support may be overwhelming enough to bring the person who has offended you to apologise. If the offender still refuses to acknowledge the error of his or her ways, you are instructed to let everybody know; and if the offender still refuses to listen, you must cast him or her out.

The list of acts that would warrant setting this process into action includes stealing, murder, coveting, revelling, drunkenness, debauchery, licentiousness, quarrelling and jealousy. These are still relevant today, and to them we would perhaps add rape, pornography, sexual abuse, and emotional and physical violence. Nothing much has really changed as far as abusive human behaviour goes in the last two thousand years. The only thing that has changed is that we have softened our processes. In the name of so-called Christian conduct we question our right to judge another person when we ourselves are sinners, adding that we must forgive 'seventy times seven' times.

Paul says that confrontation with the person who has offended you is an act of love and love is not wrong. But love costs everything and demands responsible action. This process is designed to allow an offender to say sorry, and it is this apology that frees the one who is offended to forgive the offender. Forgiveness requires the contrition of the offender towards the one who is offended. The person who has been offended is then, and only then, free to forgive the offender and reinstate the relationship.

However, modern writers on forgiveness tell us that if we do not forgive freely and perpetually then it is damaging to our spirit. The process of forgiveness has been reduced to an acceptance of the world as it is rather than the world as it should be. In the books and articles I have read about forgiveness, I am shocked at the way it has been reduced to an individual and unilateral act when it was designed originally as part of the process towards the reconciliation between two people for the good of the whole community. When forgiveness is used unwisely it acts against its original intention, and this new individual style of forgiveness is an offence against the original ideology governing the process of forgiveness. Its purpose is about community responsibility and united social action against someone who disrupts the normal flow of community interaction.

In our culture of individualism, forgiveness is used to conceal abuse on the grounds that public knowledge of the abuse would damage the reputation of the offender. This way of looking at forgiveness from an individual point of view speaks volumes about how we can twist a value to fit in with the current philosophy of individualism. Forgiveness as a unilateral act for one's own spiritual, emotional or physical health is absolutely not what forgiveness is all about. Forgiveness is about community, not individual, health. Subscribing to the view that it is healthy for the individual to forgive without engaging in the process of forgiveness is damaging to the community. This act of forgiveness hides abuse and allows the offender to keep on offending without having to engage in some analysis of the behaviour that has caused pain to another. It allows the abused to suffer twice for the offence, first for the offence itself and second in the struggle to understand why the culprit has been allowed to emerge free from blame for the incident. It is the abused person who is left struggling, gasping with the injustice of it all. It is a cheap way of covering up a problem for the sake of peace, with the consequence that it becomes a socially condoned behaviour. If offenders are not offered the opportunity to understand their offensive behaviour and are not expected to express regret, then they are free to keep on offending. Only when offenders understand the nature of their actions and the catastrophic effect their actions have had, then, and only then, can they be forgiven.

When women obey the cultural or spiritual injunction to conform to the ideology of inferiority to men, they can be subjected to violation and abuse. It is this behaviour, which is meted out to them as an inferior, that they are asked to forgive. But forgiveness on this level condones male violence towards women, because women are asked to do the 'Christian' thing and freely forgive the man who has abused them. This is not forgiveness. This is accepting the fact that the world is an ugly place where abuse is a normal occurrence. The world will remain an ugly place if the process for forgiveness and reconciliation is not put into effect. Too many women unilaterally forgive the men who abuse them in the belief that their forgiveness will heal a rift in their relationship. This sort of forgiveness is an emotional blanket that covers over an offence, hiding it from public view. Women are inclined to bear an offence in secret and in silence, which causes them terrible suffering. They may think that this is how it is supposed to be. They may talk to their friends about how offended they feel, denigrating the offenders behind their backs, but they will not go to the offenders to tell them how offended or hurt they are. By suffering in silence, they give the offenders cause to believe that they are free to continue to cause pain to others. By neglecting to confront the offenders, they deny them the opportunity to understand the nature of their actions, an opportunity that could lead to self-understanding. If the offenders are able to understand the negative impact on the relationship then they have a chance to amend their behaviour. Too often we leave out the middle bit and offer unconditional forgiveness without expecting the offenders to reflect on the action or behaviour that has caused the offence.

The church exists to ensure that justice is done and people contribute to it in the belief that it is doing this. When it does not act for justice within its own ranks and engages in self-protective behaviour, it engages in deceit. Like any other institution, the church puts itself first and the individuals within it second. The church teaches about forgiveness and the spiritual benefits this brings, but the biblical injunction to forgive 'seventy times seven' does not mean that we neglect the process of forgiveness, which is laid down clearly. The human ability to forgive comes from God, but even the forgiveness of God only happens after repentance. Forgiveness is not an unconditional act of love. It is conditional upon repentance or contrition. Forgiveness is not free. Forgiving someone without confrontation is not forgiveness, it is merely an acceptance that what happened, happened without the ultimate benefits of reconciliation.

I endured sexual abuse from a minister of the church and, without following the proper processes, the church expects me to forgive my offender unconditionally. Forgiveness as demanded by the church has to be viewed with suspicion because forgiveness is not an act of self-will. And yet the nicest people I know adhere to the belief that one should keep on forgiving 'seventy times seven'. But the process of forgiveness must be followed seventy times seven too. Blind forgiveness conceals, justifies and condones violence because the one who is violated will forgive. Without the proper process of forgiveness, justice can never be achieved. Forgiveness should never be freely offered to offenders unless they understand that their acts of violence have caused pain and they are sorry for what they have done.

SIX

Sexuality and spirituality

There is no doubt that relationships between people are becoming increasingly complex. Today's society has passed well beyond the structured order that the enforcement of social roles perpetuated for so long. Some more traditional societies have maintained this rigid social division between men and women based on reproduction and strength; but in our Western world, which we like to call modern, health technology has allowed a woman to control her pregnancies, thus increasing her life span and her opportunities for education and social participation. At the same time, aided by the women's movement in the seventies, the Western world has become increasingly liberal in its social parameters, enabling women to find an intellectual and economic role in the work place.

However, the hierarchy of the workplace has, up until now, been governed by the expectations of men. These expectations have been thrown into confusion as women have joined the professions as their intellectual equals and colleagues, and this has necessitated some change in men's working attitudes towards women. Work relationships between men and women have had to be slowly worked out through individual experience of pain, with the realisation by both sexes that the old traditions do not work any more. As expectations about behaviour in the workplace change because of the increasing numbers of women who have claimed their place there, new forms of oppression and violence towards women are revealed. These include disparity in pay, lack of communication, deprivation of information, passing the hard or unwanted jobs onto women, women working longer hours, intimidation, sexual harassment and many others.

This new violence is difficult to detect because our language has not had time to incorporate these new forms of terror. New terminology has to be found in order to expand our horizons of understanding. The occurrence of the behaviour has to be drawn into the language before we can successfully describe the fact. Until abusive behaviour is recognised and named it remains invisible and secret, or else it is turned into a joke.

When everything is in place for women to advance, and with the provision of equal education and career opportunities, why is there still something that prevents them from advancing at the rate that would be expected? There are many reasons for this. Some women do not want a career, or choose the more traditional path of caring for children. Other women want a career, but actively choose not to advance to their full potential because they do not want the stress. The power that men exercise over women in the workplace is only one among many reasons why women do not achieve.

Sexual violation of women by men is one expression of this expectation of male power. It is perhaps the most subtle, sophisticated, deliberate and cheapest form of violence towards women, and knowingly engages her at her most vulnerable and exposed core. The part of her that is the deep heart of her spirituality and sexuality is exploited and violated forever. To engage a woman at the level of her emotions when she wishes to engage at her intellectual and spiritual levels is the most insidious form of abuse. As she searches for her intellect and her spirituality she is constantly directed back to her emotions. Like the church that is struggling to deal with the dichotomy of modern and traditional practice, the woman is pulled out of kilter, away from herself, and she is denied access to her very richest resources, those that offer her integrity and wholeness. The glass ceiling that keeps a woman down is constructed from her own exploited and violated emotions.

We women have learnt much in the last twenty years. We have

talked to each other across continents and deep in time. If we genuinely desire equal participation in society, we must be aware of the ways in which we can participate equally without sacrificing our integrity. If we aim for equality with men, our sights are set on a different goal. Seeking equality with men implies that we are not already equal and that to achieve equality is an upward movement. This aim for equality asks us to be like men, and we must ask if this is really what we women want. To be equal with men would mean that we would have to deny our emotions and our values, in other words our femininity—that which makes us women. It would mean an end to peace in order to engage in conflict.

It would be far more advantageous for society if we brought our values and our ethics out of the private and into the public sphere. In this way we would achieve a more equitable society where men and women are on an equal footing without either sex having to compromise their integrity or values. Women do not have to buy into a 'man's world'. We can do what we are best at, which is being different from men and demanding that this difference be respected as essential for the good of the whole.

How can we do this? It is easy to say what we do not want. It is much harder to find out what we do want. How can the reality and the vision meet and become one? It is more likely that, when the reality and the vision do meet, there will be conflict and crisis rather than unity. The vision of what we expect the world should be like is very different from the reality we encounter in everyday life. Yet, in spite of the reality that constantly confronts us, we carry around in our heads the vision of a perfect world where all our expectations are met. And even though the reality does not come within reach of the vision, we do not make the vision conform with the reality of everyday; instead we manufacture a huge amount of energy to attempt to change and shape the reality we encounter into that vision. At the very moment when we encounter the reality without the vision we have lost hope and have become out of touch with our spirituality, for it is our spirituality that drives us onwards in hope. There has to be a reason for the crisis we experience when the reality and the vision clash. I want to explore some of these reasons in terms of sexuality and spirituality.

✣

I have always wondered why religious teaching represses sexuality in favour of spirituality? The Bible speaks abundantly about sexuality, both in the Old Testament and in the New. Let us take the issue of adultery, for instance, and follow it through the two Testaments. I choose adultery because the concept has undergone enormous change in the development of society over thousands of years. Now, apart from cultural disapproval, there is no secular law against adultery. However, society's disapproval stems from the biblical laws against adultery as they are written in the Ten Commandments in Exodus 20: 14 and 17. In verse 14 the commandment not to commit adultery follows the commandment not to kill, and is followed by the commandment not to steal. In Moses' law it would appear that adultery is a life and death matter, only marginally less serious than murder but more serious than theft. Its position between killing and stealing appears anomalous to us now, since our law says that murder and theft are criminal offences whereas adultery is not. Yet in those days it was taken extremely seriously.

Why was adultery considered to be such a critical issue? Adultery was a property issue. It was not about sentiments of fidelity, loyalty or love of one's wife, but a matter of inheritance of property. Common theory has it that men needed to know that the children born to their partner were their own children for the purposes of inheritance. In modern parlance, one could say that adultery was considered to be intergenerational theft. A man could impregnate another man's wife with the result that his son would inherit the property of another man. Instead of fighting or killing for property, it was a known activity to take it by other more devious means. The injunction against adultery tells us how men throughout history have kept wealth and property in their own hands to maintain a patriarchal society. Men were directed to keep their sexual distance from other men's wives so that the ownership of property could remain in the hands of one family; this family would also retain the power conferred upon them by this ownership, hence the importance of sons.

Looking behind the law, not at what it says but rather at what it does not say, we can see that the law implies that women were considered to be the vehicle for male property rights. The woman herself had no rights, since she could not own property, and was not regarded as fully human, since she was the possession of a man. So she was not included in the law against adultery. But, since her womb was the means by which the theft could be perpetrated, this had its hazards. Hence the need for the law.

In verse 17 the command not to desire a neighbour's wife is included with the command not to desire his house, his male or female slave, his ox, his donkey, or anything that belongs to him. In this list of desirables, the house is considered to be a more important possession than his wife because the house precedes the wife, who comes second in the list. To act out the desire that led to adultery was evidently a great deal more serious than the desire itself, although even the merest hint of desire is considered an offence.

There are two important points to note. First, it appears that the Ten Commandments are written for men, not for women, otherwise it would have included the command not to desire a neighbour's husband. Second, it is clear that a woman was owned by a man in exactly the same way that a house, a slave, or a donkey was his possession. The command in verse 17 clearly indicates that adultery only applies to men, because women are subject to men in the same way that animals are.

The Mosaic law is further explored in the New Testament, where the dimension of property inheritance has disappeared and adultery is made to stand alone as a sin in itself. It is made clear in Mark 7:21 that adultery is an evil intention that comes from the human heart and defiles a person. Matthew 5:27 agrees with Mark when Jesus says: 'You have heard that it was said, "You shall not commit adultery." But I say to you that everyone who looks at a woman with lust has already committed adultery with her in his heart.' Rather more complex is the injunction concerning divorce in verse 31, where Jesus is made to say, 'But I say to you that anyone who divorces his wife, except on the ground of unchastity, causes her to commit adultery; and whoever marries a divorced woman commits adultery.' It is strange that a woman commits adultery just because she is divorced. But in 18:9 the confusion about who exactly commits adultery is clarified. 'Whoever divorces his wife, except for unchastity, and marries another commits adultery.' We note that these commands in the New Testament tell men to control their sexuality rather than women.

Paul in 1 Corinthians says that people who engage in sexual immorality—adulterers, male prostitutes, fornicators and sodomites—will not inherit the Kingdom of God, which brings us back to the issue of inheritance. Why male prostitutes and not female prostitutes? Is this a legitimising of female prostitution for men? In Hebrews 13:4 this same list of people are threatened with God's judgement, which is punishment meted out by men.

This punishment is described in a metaphor of Jerusalem's infidelity to Yahweh in Ezekiel 16:38, but strangely, it is a punishment for women, not men, even though the laws are directed at the behaviour of men. It is worthwhile reading the text for its sheer violence against women.

> I will judge you as women who commit adultery and shed blood are judged, and bring blood upon you in wrath and jealousy. I will

> deliver you into their hands, and they shall throw down your platform and break down your lofty places; they shall strip you of your clothes and take your beautiful objects and leave you naked and bare. They shall bring up a mob against you, and they shall stone you and cut you to pieces with their swords. They shall burn your houses and execute judgements on you in the sight of many women; I will stop you from playing the whore...so I will satisfy my fury on you, and my jealousy shall turn away from you.

It would appear that women bear the brunt of men's desires to the extent that they are held responsible for adultery and are punished for it by men. Men did not appear to be punished to the same extent as women. Genesis 38 tells of the punishment meted out to adulterous women when Judah, Tamar's father-in-law, orders her death by burning for committing adultery. When Tamar reveals that she is pregnant with Judah's child she is released and allowed to live. No punishment is brought upon the head of Judah for committing adultery, since he is the one who controls the situation by ordering Tamar's death for the same sin that he has committed. He releases her from her death sentence for the sake of his own child. David, on the other hand, in 2 Samuel 1:14, commits adultery with Bathsheba and upon confession is freed from the death sentence. His new-born son, conceived in this adulterous relationship, dies in his stead.

The most extraordinary story of all occurs in John 8:3 where the woman caught in the act of adultery (note that the man, who, I imagine, was also caught in the act of adultery since a woman cannot commit adultery on her own, is excluded from this confrontation) is brought to Jesus by a group of men who ask him whether they should stone her to death or not. Jesus' response is 'Let anyone among you who is without sin be the first to throw a stone at her.' When they heard this the men went away, one by one, and Jesus was left alone with the woman standing before him. Jesus straightened up and said to her, 'Woman, where are they? Has no-one condemned you?' She said, 'No one, sir.' And Jesus said, 'Neither do I condemn you. Go your way, and from now on do not sin again.'

John is the only gospel that offers a merciful solution. From this we can deduce several matters. In a case of adultery, only the woman sins. However, on the basis that everyone sins, she is not condemned to death. The adulterous man wins both ways. The woman is labelled the sinner in an adulterous relationship, not the man, so he is exempt from judgement on that count. Also, since he is a sinner in general, like everyone else, he is once again free from judgement. Thus men's so-called 'red-bloodedness' is given cultural and religious acceptance.

From a woman's point of view, it is clear that, although we may not initiate sexual advances, we are still held responsible for the man's sexual advances. In Muslim countries the women are covered from head to toe in order that men may not see them and be tempted. In the Western Christian world, women are encouraged to display as much of themselves as possible. The Western world allows men to gaze upon women and to be tempted. But desire itself is considered sinful, so the responsibility for men's desire is placed firmly on the woman.

This is made very clear in Genesis 3:12, when the man blames the woman for his sin: 'The man said, "The woman whom you gave to be with me, she gave me fruit from the tree, and I ate."' The man not only blames the woman for his desire, he also blames God for creating the woman in the first place. There is an insidious strand throughout that men are never responsible for their actions.

These teachings about adultery in the Bible appear to condone men's sexual behaviour, but not women's. Men are unconditionally forgiven for any breaches of conduct, but women must pay the price for the men. The price that a woman pays is high, for it appears that she must take full responsibility both for herself and for the behaviour of men. When a relationship occurs that is out of kilter in the eyes of the church, forgiveness is given unconditionally to men but not to women. Men blame women for their actions even though men are the cause of the sin in the first place. The more modern and liberal approach to adultery is that if two people are consenting partners in any relationship then it is acceptable. The catch in this formula is when an imbalance of power exists in the relationship. When this imbalance of power is present between two people, when one person has authority over the other, consent can never be freely given by the powerless partner.

✣

Having examined the ambivalent attitude in the Bible towards men's and women's sexuality, let us now look at an essay called 'Sexuality and Spirituality' (in *Women of Spirit*, Hilton Press) written by the Reverend Peg Riley in 1996. She endeavours, in a unique, honest and personal exploration of sexuality and spirituality, to explore her own inner being in order to discover the difference, or rather the similarities, between these two strands of being. She offers us the understanding that sexuality and spirituality are both, together and inseparably, the creative mainspring of each human being that makes each one of us unique in our individuality. Both emanate from the same source of existence and make us whole people. If we have sexuality without spirituality then we are not fully human, for sexuality with spirituality offers a sacred dimension to our relationships. If we have spirituality without sexuality then we are not incarnate beings. When spirituality has gone, leaving an empty house, then the sexual urge becomes the primary force and can wreak havoc and become destructive. Sexuality and spirituality, as the two primary strands of our being, must exist together side by side, but always in some tension. When there is too much tension between the two, one must give way to the other, spirituality to sexuality, or sexuality to spirituality.

Riley concedes that both are very difficult to put into words and are difficult to tell apart. She does not say to herself 'Now I shall be spiritual' or 'Now I shall be sexual', for she admits that both are beyond the control of her will or her intellect. She says:

> Both these concepts speak about the creative energy that is my being...I cannot conceive of 'spirituality' or 'sexuality' as poles on continuums or as points of definition, to say easily 'this is that' or 'that is this', but rather as emotive and physical expressions of attitudes, thoughts and feelings. Even under analysis it is not easy to say that this part of me is sexual and this part of me is spiritual. For the two are integrally bound together in the deepest core of being, highlighting, deepening and enhancing other experiences.

She says that the judgement of a sexual or a spiritual mode of communication comes not from her own perception but from the perception of others, who claim that they are able to receive communication in whatever form from her, from their own levels of response. She claims that because she acts out of her own integrity, as a whole person, people respond to her from their own sexuality or spirituality. In other words it is the perception of the other that categorises her communication, either by words or by touch, to be one or the other.

Riley says that although both spirituality and sexuality are beyond the intellect and the will, both serve to give rise to the whole persona. She believes that her own integrity, which includes self-knowledge, and her own ability to love and be loved is primary and paramount. Yet she expresses her fear at revealing her innermost thoughts because of the assumptions and judgements of prejudice and condemnation, and understands that such a revelation requires a degree of self-knowledge, assurance and trust of the other person that they will withhold their judgements.

> We are vulnerable to the taboos in society which say to us, 'don't talk about sexuality because it is dirty', and 'spirituality is pure'. We

> cannot speak about these things for fear of breaking the taboos. Sexuality and spirituality are both about being in relationship. Relationship with God, with self and with others. This is where the confusion and difficulty in separating these aspects of me can happen. They are both the very closest interpersonal interactions that humans can experience.

Riley asks of the tradition of women in the church

> ...have we suppressed our sexuality in the name of spirituality in order to be acceptable to an institution that cannot handle the two as one and which feels the strong vibrations of women's sexuality as a disturbing threat? As a woman of the church I have had experiences of being judged, rejected and abused from other people's perceptions of my sexuality and spirituality...these experiences of judgement do not define me for I know that I am loved and I know that I am a loving person.

There is no doubt that the church has always repressed sexuality in favour of spirituality and it is true to say that women struggle to maintain the balance between their sexuality and spirituality in the church, which has strong traditions in favour of men's sexuality but not women's sexuality. But when we read Peg Riley's analysis of the two as being inseparable, we begin to understand that it is not only difficult to suppress one essence of being in favour of the other but impossible. By repressing one essential part of being, people become so severely unbalanced in their inner being that they must come to the point of denying their own humanity.

We know that sexuality will not be suppressed in favour of spirituality. The Roman Catholic church has shown us time and time again that celibacy does not work and that the resulting sexual predation of men, women and children by priests would indicate that it is not a healthy lifestyle. As a logical step from this, we can be forgiven for assuming that since priests in Protestant churches are able to marry and have children the matter of destructive sexuality would not arise, assuming of course that their sexuality is contained within limits of normalcy. What we fail to understand is that the spiritual creativity of any individual must of necessity draw its energy or images from the other essential strand of being, that of sexuality. However much anyone denies this extraordinary insight, it is important that we look at the reasons for our humanity in order to understand sexuality and spirituality.

It is a philosophical argument as to whether spirituality or sexuality is our primary driving force. When we think about sexuality as the primary motivation of life, we are taking our created existence, our life, as a given without exploring our origins or understanding that there was a time when we were not. By understanding our sexuality as primary, we are taking our aliveness for granted. When, however, we take one step backwards from the principle that life is a given, an *a priori* truth, we move into how we are given life, rather than why we are given life.

Christian theologians claim that all creation is brought about by God, that humanity is the crowning glory of creation and that our tangible and visible fact of existence is the key element of life, which offers sufficient proof that our spirituality is primary to our sexuality. Not only Christian stories, but stories in every faith and culture relate their understanding about how the human species came into being. Christians and Jews say that our life-spirit was breathed into us by the breath of God and that we emerged from the earth itself. Greek and Roman stories tell how the gods came to earth and mated with earth women. Now, evolutionists claim that human beings developed from apes through a process of evolution. In the end it does not really matter one way or another how we came to have life. The real point is that somehow and for some reason we are gifted with life. The real argument is centred on whether this life source, which we will call the 'how' of existence, or the biological drive to perpetuate the species, which we can call the 'why' of existence, is primary to existence.

Sexuality and spirituality constitute the how and the why of our existence and both claim to be the essence of life. And both are. Our spirituality and our sexuality emerge from the same source of our being as different strands, which are so closely intertwined that it is difficult at times to distinguish between them as they emerge in patterns of behaviour. Sexuality is our biological reason for being, our identity as humans. Human beings, along with all of creation, have a biological urge to perpetuate the species. It is this single factor which aligns us with creation in partnership. Our sexual instinct is the strongest drive that we have. All animals and plants are involved with the perpetuation of their own species. As partners in creation we cannot in all honesty claim that we do not have similar primitive urges to mate. One group of scientists would say that our sexuality is our basic reason for living, intellectual potential aside, and that everything we do is an impulse towards procreation. Whether we believe that or not, the most important question which emerges is whether our sexuality can be made subservient to our spirituality or our spirituality made subservient to our sexuality.

If we look to the church to find the answer to this question, we see that the church is governed by conservative traditions that do not make for an easy answer. The church is seen to be a repository of human values and beliefs. The values of goodness, kindness, love, faith, charity and humility contribute greatly to the structures of society, offering behavioural norms and standards to any community. Even in times of tumultuous change the church has clung to its self-made and self-perpetuating conservative values of patriarchy that have enabled it to survive for the past two thousand years in the belief that these values are divinely ordained by God. Because of the church's influence over society, these values have become cultural values. Because the needs of the people have changed, the church has to decide whether to change with the people or to become more authoritarian in order to preserve its traditions. I believe that the institution of the church has survived long enough not to be afraid of change and that one of its ongoing tasks is to respond to any challenge in a spirit of openness and honesty.

However, some of these values are not so much God-given as man-made for the ongoing supremacy of male power and control. It is inevitable that the conservative stance of the church and its traditions will be challenged by educated women who experience discomfort with its male exclusiveness. The so-called 'eternal' values are being called into question by women who seek a place within the church, which continues to advocate male primacy. Feminist theologians wrestle with a male-based spirituality that says women are subordinate to men. Their task is to reinterpret the Bible so that women can have an equal share in the goods that the church has to offer. But the tectonic plates of the church grind slowly, too slowly for some, as it seeks ways to incorporate modern thinking with traditional practice and the perception is that the church is reluctant to change.

The concern about the malaise within the church offers us an opportunity to remind the church of its own values. As members of the church, we are empowered to invite the church to reflect on the purpose of its existence and at the same time to ensure that its priests, ministers and pastors are responsible for the promotion of those values and are to be held accountable to the institution should they fall short of their own mission.

Conclusion

It is interesting now to look back and see why all of this happened. What ought to have been a simple process became a nightmare even though the process was legislated for in the statutes and canons of the church. We thought we were being responsible members of a community by alerting the bishop to the fact that there was a problem. I suppose we were naïve. After all, we were complaining about sexual deviancy within the church. We certainly did not expect that finding a resolution to the problem would take the years that it did. We trusted the church to manage the situation for us, having managed as best as we could for as long as we could. We were aware of R's wife and children, and for some years we had respected his situation far more deeply than he had ever respected our individual situations, our children and our husbands. We had given him the benefit of the doubt for too long. We respected his ability to establish theological education and his position of seniority within the church. His charisma and vision made him a popular man. But we had to balance that against his known propensity to prey sexually on young female students and since the college was going to accept female students we were fearful that they would find it difficult to cope with such a manipulative man. It was for those university students and for the churchwomen that we made the final decision to complain about his nefarious activities.

When we filed our complaints in writing we did expect to be believed. We thought of ourselves as mature, responsible people who were prepared to risk revealing this man's sexually predatory nature towards women. We thought that because we were ordained and well educated we would be taken seriously. We also believed that if only one of us complained, that one would be disadvantaged. We felt it was safer to complain jointly and we hoped, by the sheer strength of numbers, that we would be believed.

We had no idea that the church would rise up against us and become so defensive, offensive and abusive about our action. We did not anticipate that the church would wash its hands of the matter and hand it over to the board of governors of the college. We had no idea that the college board would disbelieve us either, especially since we felt that we were doing them a favour by complaining about a situation that had the potential to severely damage the reputation of the college. We would never have guessed that the board would ask no questions but merely accept R's resignation with regret, apologise to him for our complaints and give him a golden handshake.

With the mismanagement of two institutions the process went wildly out of control. The church stepped back and allowed the board to be seen to do the dirty work. The board did not investigate our complaints, sacked the theological teachers, and restructured themselves. The gossip machine started up and rumours abounded. The men and many women took R's side and believed him to be the innocent victim of an orchestrated plot.

We had tried to protect women from sexual abuse. Instead, we revealed the church's contempt for women and its fear of sexuality. As in nuclear warfare, we were contaminated by the fallout and we were thought to contaminate the church. We suffered the rage of a wounded worldwide institution. We had 'told' on them. We were whistleblowers. Unwittingly, we had uncovered their game, thrown their blankets off, and, like lovers caught in the act, they turned guiltily upon us and blamed the women. Two mighty forces clashed, male against female. All of us lost our innocence and gained more knowledge than we knew what to do with.

We now know that when women stand up in the face of evil and desire the good, men seek to destroy us. But we can never be destroyed, for we are the creators of men and men know this. When women are threatened by our sons, we sink into the earth, which is our refuge, and wait for our time to come. The time has come and we stretch out our hands to receive it, to accept it gratefully in the spirit of good, in the spirit of peace and in the spirit of everlasting life. We will never be conquered. Our bodies are the earth and the sky, our fertility is our creativity, and our growth is inexorable, patient, resilient, and persistent against the odds. And again we rise to flourish with beauty, revelling in the goodness of the earth, which is ours and which we boldly claim for ourselves. For now we know the truth and we will not forget.

Postscript

The other day my telephone rang. It was my barrister friend, N, asking whether I wanted the matter of R's portrait brought before the board of governors of the college. Before I agreed to this proposal, he carefully explained that, in doing so, he would be acting in the capacity of my advocate and not as a member of the board. I understood his position clearly, although I was uncertain how a member of the board could be a member of the board and yet not be a member of the board. After he had clarified his position, I told him that the portrait of R was no longer a problem, since I had written this book and would now prefer R to remain hanging in the college dining room. There was a pause on the other end of the line. Our conversation ended on the understanding that he would talk to the board about the portrait and he would tell them that I had written this book.

The day after the board had met, he rang me early in the morning to report back on the board's reactions. He explained that there was now a new board and that things at the college were running very smoothly. I expressed delight at this. He said that very few people looked at a line-up of portraits of stuffy old men on the walls of the dining room. I disagreed with this since I, along with many others, enjoy looking at portraits on dining room walls and I did not agree with his suggestion that the portraits were invisible.

He tried again. He explained that there are two very active women board members who were horrified at the treatment that we had received and were willing to make amends. These women had requested that I meet with them, and they would employ a QC to act as a mediator cum conciliator. I said it was a shame that the board had not done this ten years ago. He agreed with me and said that the board was willing to make amends for their past actions. I asked why, since I could not understand what amends could be made after so long that would even touch the pain. N repeated that it was a new board and that if I talked to the students I would be amazed at the change in the place. I replied that I still used the theological library at the college and had no fear of the place. On the contrary, I said, I went there quite often and was well aware of the changes. Privately, I thought that I did not have to worry about the principal pursuing me any more.

At last, in desperation, N came out with the real intention of his call, which was that the board were worried about the detrimental effect that my book would have on the reputation of the college. I carefully said to him that the board should have thought about this before they acted in the way they did. He hesitated and said that the most important issue was that they wanted to meet with me, four of them with a mediator, to talk things over. He said that he had requested that the board pay for the services of a mediator. It was left that I would ring the man whose name had been put forward to mediate.

I rang him and we discussed the matter. I allowed him to conduct the conversation and realised that the most important matter on the board's mind was the reputation of the college as a result of this book. He was not so concerned about reconciliation as about mediation. It was not so much the acute distress and loss of careers of so many people that they were willing to apologise or make amends for. What they were concerned about was the loss of their own reputation. We talked about his suitability to be a mediator in the light of our professional connections and friendship, since I was very concerned that he might feel a conflict of interest. At this he responded that he had been asked to act as counsel for the board, to advise them what to do. I was quite confused, since I had been led to believe that the board was paying for his services to act for the complainants. We left it that I would consider it and call him back.

That night I rang Patricia Allan, now the minister at Durham Street Methodist Church. I outlined the situation to her, and she said she would be delighted to attend such a meeting and would make sure she was available. I rang another complainant, who expressed some reservation at such a meeting and said she would think it over. Another complainant said that she would be there with knobs on. Another suggested that the women meet together first to discuss it. Ten years have passed and not one person who was involved in this case has thrown away the letters and newspaper cuttings. In fact, it is still so alive in their minds that they are prepared to put their daily lives aside to sally forth again.

How could the board make amends? After eleven years the career paths of some of the participants tell their own story. Three members of our group, who had participated out of a strong sense of justice and not because they had been sexually abused by R, were unable to find employment again in the Diocese of Christchurch. Rev Patricia Allan, who led us so ably in the process of seeking justice, was later somewhat reluctantly appointed to the newly created hierarchical position of Diocesan Mission Co-ordinator. (She was told that the church was worried about what some of the men would think!) Within two and a half years this position was disestablished without any adequate explanation except the job review noted that some people found it difficult to work with the incumbent because of her involvement in professional misconduct issues. Patricia told the Bishop and Vicar General that it felt like the ultimate payback in the R saga. In spite of applying for every vacant possible position in the Diocese of Christchurch, after nearly a year Patricia was still not in employment. She, in fact, needed the year to recover from the terrible consequences of standing with those who had been abused by R. Whilst still holding the Bishop's license in the Anglican Church she is now very happily leading a vibrant Methodist Church as a Methodist minister.

The four complainants have had varying success in their careers. One was side-lined for many years as a school chaplain. Another was unable to find work at all within the Presbyterian Church and has been forced to make a career change. I was forced to resign my position as a voluntary priest. One of the members of the board of governors, who had breached confidentiality by telling his wife who had then caused a violent schism in my family, was also the vicar's warden in my parish, where I had worked for many years in a voluntary capacity. He and the vicar forced my resignation from this position so that I was unable to function, even in a voluntary capacity, in my own parish. I put my name forward for about half a dozen parishes within the diocese and was turned down each time. I wondered why I had been turned down so often. When I worked as a locum in one of the parishes that I had applied for, it was revealed to me why my applications had not been successful. The wardens in this parish asked me why I had not applied to minister in their parish. I replied that I had and that I had been turned down. They said that my name had not been given to them by the bishop. The nominators had repeatedly asked the bishop if there were only two applicants for the position and asked if any women had applied. The bishop had reassured them that there were only two applicants and that no women had applied. The nominators asked him if he was absolutely sure, and he said that he was absolutely sure.

When I reflected upon the number of ills caused by the board's lack of action on the matter, I wondered if the board could ever make amends for what they had done to us. I wondered how a board could make amends for the schism in my family, or for my forced withdrawal from my parish after six years of training for priesthood, or for allowing rumours and lies to circulate about all of us. I wondered how a board could even apologise when some of the original board members were still on the board.

As I pondered over these things, I realised that their chief concern was not about us, but about their own reputation. I began to understand that they wanted to stop the publication of this book. They had taken away my career, my self-esteem and now they want to take away this story. I wondered if they might offer me money to withdraw it.

I began to see that they had attempted to protect themselves in the beginning by treating us in the way that they did. Ten years ago they chose one course of action out of a number of possible ones. If they acted out of what they thought was integrity then, they must accept accountability now. If they sue me for libel, I have told no lies. They took a cheap and easy way out for themselves without considering the consequences for us.

✣

Recently I received a telephone call from a person who had been on the board ten years ago and is still a board member. We talked. I was surprised to hear him say that R had manipulated a board constituted of lawyers, judges, QCs and university staff, and that they had never asked R about the reason for our written complaints when these complaints were received by the board. R had taken his lawyer along, and the lawyer had read out a statement that said that R understood that he had lost the confidence of the board and that he refuted all the complaints laid against him.

The other surprise was hearing that the board had also been manipulated by the bishop. The bishop had informed the complainants that their complaints to him as the head of the diocese were not valid on account of the fact that the church did not employ R, and we were requested to make our complaints again to the board of governors. The odd factor about this was that the chairman of the board of governors of the college was the bishop himself. He informed the board that the church had stripped R of his church positions and that everything was under control. The bishop had also advocated that R retain his position as principal of the college. However, because members of the board had experienced difficulties with the principal in the past, the board decided to use the women's complaints as a means of forcing R's resignation. We were the scapegoats in another drama about which we knew nothing.

✣

We have had two meetings with four members of the board of the college. Both meetings lasted for three hours. At the first meeting we put before them our grievances against the board and called for compensation of $60,000 each on the grounds that, since they gave R this amount in return for his resignation, they should be prepared to give the same to us. At the second meeting they told us that they were not able to offer us any monetary compensation but would write us a letter of apology and also would write to the General Synod of the Anglican Church of New Zealand and each of the bishops, telling them that the church handled the whole affair badly and chastising them for withholding information from the board. They also offered to facilitate a meeting with members of the board, the complainants and our avocate, and the church.

It is interesting to watch an institution reflect on its own history and begin to deal with it. I am only mildly interested in the possibility that the board may ask me to lay down my pen. I have no obedience left in me now, no desire to please. I suppose they think that if they apologise, I will forgive them. But if I am to forgive them they must first comprehend the full extent of the damage they have caused to so many people. The best that they can do now is forgive themselves for ignoring basic human rights and resolve to be more vigilant in these matters in the future.

Finally, what I am able to offer them is this. I am able to offer them my compassion for the dilemma they have brought upon themselves. But in the end, they have to be accountable for their actions, the same as all of us. There are no exemptions from accountability. I can offer them some insights into their own actions so that they can learn that there are other ways of doing things rather than destroying other people and that, in order to be fully human, they too must humble themselves and brush the dust off their own knees. No one else can do that for them.

For myself, I desire nothing. My health has gone. I have lost eighteen years of my life. I have nothing left to lose now except my integrity and my wisdom and I have no intention of letting them go, for they mean everything to me. But they have everything to lose. Without integrity, none of us, neither individuals nor institutions, can stand and be counted. Without integrity, we are complicit accomplices in a world that takes every opportunity to be corrupt and dishonest. Without integrity, good cannot exist alongside evil and we can easily and innocently slip into the traps that evil sets for us.

In the end, this is not about a little board of governors of a university hostel at the end of the world. The board was merely a puppet in the hands of the church, a poor puppet, a blind puppet, a puppet that had no idea of the singular machinations of this great machinery of the church, which has survived for so long because of its ability to manipulate and deceive. It is really a story about the church and its devious attitudes and practices towards women. The condition of entry into the church is compliance to the world of men. R was merely a sick emanation, a product of the church, whom the church chose to protect against all his victims and who reflects the church's image back to itself. In protecting R the church protected its own power, as it has over the centuries, as in the Inquisition that condemned innocent people to death and the countless wars that are fought in the name of God. The church must bear the pain it has inflicted on men and women for so many centuries.

Recommended Reading

DEANS, Louise M., ed. *Women of Spirit*. Privately published by Hilton Press, 1996.

DOWRICK, Stephanie. *Forgiveness and Other Acts of Love*. Viking Penguin, 1997.

FORTUNE, Marie M. *Is Nothing Sacred? The Story of a Pastor, the Women He Sexually Abused, and the Congregation He Nearly Destroyed*. HarperSanFrancisco, 1989.

FRENCH, Marilyn. *Beyond Power: On Women, Men and Morals*. Abacus, 1986.

GARNER, Helen. *The First Stone: Some Questions About Sex and Power*. Picador, 1995.

HITE, Shere. 'Women as Revolutionary Agents of Change' in *The Hite Reports: Sexuality, Love and Emotion*. Sceptre, 1993.

LERNER, Harriet Goldhor. *The Dance of Anger: A Woman's Guide to Changing the Patterns of Intimate Relationships*. Harper and Row, 1985.

MALTZ, Wendy. *The Sexual Healing Journey: A Guide for Survivors of Sexual Abuse*. HarperPerennial, 1992.

PECK, M. Scott. *People of the Lie: The Hope for Healing Human Evil*. Arrow Books, 1990.

RUSSELL, Letty M., ed. *Feminist Interpretation of the Bible*. Basil Blackwell, 1985.

RUTTER, Peter. *Sex in the Forbidden Zone: When Men in Power – Therapists, Doctors, Clergy, Teachers and others – Betray Women's Trust*. Unwin Paperbacks, 1990.

SCHAEF, Ann Wilson. *When Society Becomes an Addict*. Harper & Row, 1987.

SHEEHEY, Gail. *Passages: Predictable Crises of Adult Life*. Bantam Books, 1977.

SPRETNAK, Charlene, ed. *The Politics of Women's Spirituality: Essays on the rise of spiritual power within the feminist movement*. Anchor Books, Doubleday, 1982.